Also available in Twayne's Studies in Short Fiction Series

Twayne's Studies in Short Fiction

Gordon Weaver, General Editor
Oklahoma State University

WILLA CATHER
Courtesy of the Bettmann Archive.

WILLA CATHER

————— *A Study of the Short Fiction* —

Loretta Wasserman
Grand Valley State University

TWAYNE PUBLISHERS • BOSTON
A Division of G. K. Hall & Co.

Twayne's Studies in Short Fiction Series, No. 19

Copyright 1991 by G. K. Hall & Co.
All rights reserved.
Published by Twayne Publishers
A division of G. K. Hall & Co.
70 Lincoln Street
Boston, Massachusetts 02111

Copyediting supervised by Barbara Sutton.
Book production and design by Janet Z. Reynolds.
Typeset by Compset, Inc., Beverly, Massachusetts.

First published 1991.
10 9 8 7 6 5 4 3 2 1

The paper used in this publication meets the minimum requirements
of American National Standard for Information Sciences—Permanence
of Paper for Printed Library Materials, ANSI Z39.48-1984. ∞™

Printed and bound in the United States of America.

Library of Congress Cataloging-in-Publication Data

Wasserman, Loretta.
    Willa Cather : a study of the short fiction / Loretta Wasserman.
        p.   cm. — (Twayne's studies in short fiction ; no. 19)
    Includes bibliographical references (p.   ) and index.
    ISBN 0-8057-8330-X (alk. paper)
    1. Cather, Willa, 1873–1947—Criticism and interpretation.
    2. Short story.   I. Title.   II. Series.
    PS3505.A87Z937   1991
    813'.52—dc20   90-5149

For Irving, Adam, Gale, and Jessica
and
In Memory of my Parents
Lawrence and Inez Odland Rowe

Contents

Contents

PART 3. THE CRITICS

Preface

In preparing this introductory study of Willa Cather's short stories, I have had in mind the student or general reader who has been attracted to Cather through one of the stories—probably "Paul's Case" or "Neighbour Rosicky"—and wants to explore her accomplishment in this form. In short, I do not assume a familiarity with the novels. Such a sharp division between genres, although essentially artificial, allows us to look at the stories with a fresh eye and to follow thematic clues and make stylistic juxtapositions without recourse to settled assumptions.

My organization is roughly chronological, but I depart from this order in two places. In the opening chapter's discussion of Cather's affinity for the techniques and concerns of modernism, I use as examples two stories from very different periods: "The Enchanted Bluff," from 1909, and "Before Breakfast," written in the late forties at the close of Cather's life. Chapter 3, "Four Love Stories," is thematic, considering stories written at various times. Moreover, within the chronological framework I do not survey all of the stories—sixty-two, by most counts—as Marilyn Arnold has already done in her admirable *Willa Cather's Short Fiction*; rather, my aim has been to focus on the most challenging works, those responsive to a variety of critical approaches.

Cather herself was a somewhat vacillating critic of her stories. When she prepared a library edition of her works in the thirties, she was too severe, leaving out most of her early stories. On the other hand, the three collections she brought out herself, *The Troll Garden*, *Youth and the Bright Medusa*, and the wonderful *Obscure Destinies*, not only contain the best of her stories, but also show care in arrangement. I consider the stories in these collections together, as they appeared.

Part 1 of this study, then, introduces Cather as a short story writer—her influences, her aesthetic, her thematic preoccupations—and offers interpretive readings of the stories that by increasingly common consent are likely to remain significant. The aim of part 2, "The Writer," is to provide a less mediated view of the author. In it I rely on an excerpt from a memoir by a close friend, four interviews Cather gave in the early years of her success, and one of Cather's own essays on the craft of writing. Part 3 is a sample of current criticism.

Cather's compressed, allusive style—what she called the ability to "unfurnish," so that "all that one has suppressed and cut away is there to the reader's consciousness as much as if it were in type"[1]—is admirably suited to the modern short story. My goal is to demonstrate that in the best of her stories she achieves the economy of effect she believed essential in all imaginative art and that these stories reward the attention such art demands. It must be admitted that Cather has not yet been placed in the front ranks of the story writers of her time. It is my view that she belongs there.

Note

1. "On the Art of Fiction," in *Willa Cather on Writing: Critical Studies on Writing as an Art* (1949; Lincoln: University of Nebraska Press, 1988), 102.

Acknowledgments

I acknowledge with thanks permission to reprint material from the following sources:

From *Willa Cather Living* by Edith Lewis. Copyright 1953 by Edith Lewis. Reprinted by permission of Alfred A. Knopf, Inc.

"Willa Cather Talks of Work." Reprinted from *Willa Cather in Person: Interviews, Speeches, and Letters*, selected and edited by L. Brent Bohlke, by permission of University of Nebraska Press. © 1986 by the University of Nebraska Press.

"Willa Cather" by Eleanor Hinman. Reprinted by permission from the *Lincoln Sunday Star*.

"How Willa Cather Found Herself" by Eva Mahoney. Reprinted by permission from the *Omaha World-Herald*.

"Menace to Culture in Cinema and Radio Seen by Miss Cather." Reprinted from *Willa Cather in Person: Interviews, Speeches, and Letters*, selected and edited by L. Brent Bohlke, by permission of University of Nebraska Press. © 1986 by the University of Nebraska Press.

"The Novel Démeublé," from *Willa Cather on Writing: Critical Studies on Writing as an Art*. Copyright 1949 by the Executors of the Estate of Willa Cather. Reprinted by permission of Alfred A. Knopf, Inc.

"Willa Cather's Children of Grace" by John J. Murphy. Reprinted from the *Willa Cather Pioneer Memorial Newsletter* 28, no. 3. © 1984 by the Willa Cather Pioneer Memorial and Educational Foundation. Reprinted by permission.

"Nordic Mythology in Willa Cather's 'The Joy of Nelly Deane'" by Joan Wylie Hall. Reprinted from *Studies in Short Fiction* 26, no. 3, by permission of Newberry College.

"Caesar and the Artist in Willa Cather's 'Coming, Aphrodite!'" by Alice Hall Petry. Reprinted from *Studies in Short Fiction* 23, no. 3, by permission of Newberry College.

"Pittsburgh and the Conflict of Values: Mixed Melody," from *Willa Cather's Short Fiction* by Marilyn Arnold (Ohio University Press, 1984). Reprinted with permission of Ohio University Press, Athens.

"*Obscure Destinies*: Unalterable Realities," from *The Voyage Perilous: Willa Cather's Romanticism* by Susan J. Rosowski. Reprinted by permission of University of Nebraska Press. © 1986 by the University of Nebraska Press.

Photograph of Willa Cather reading courtesy of The Bettmann Archive.

Earlier versions of my discussion of Bergson and Cather appeared in "The Music of Time: Henri Bergson and Willa Cather," *American Literature* 57, no. 2 (1985), and in "William James, Henri Bergson, and Remembered Time," in *Approaches to Teaching Cather's "My Ántonia,"* ed. Susan J. Rosowski (Modern Language Association of America, 1989). An earlier version of parts of chapter 5 appeared in "Willa Cather's 'The Old Beauty' Reconsidered," *Studies in American Fiction* 16, no. 2 (1988). Parts of chapter 2 appeared in "Is Cather's Paul a Case?" *Modern Fiction Studies* (1990).

I am indebted to a number of persons for their interest in this study, but chiefly to Susan J. Rosowski, who read the first three chapters in manuscript and saved me from numerous blunders. In fact, I may say that she has been the sponsor of this book, though the inadequacies of execution are of course my own. Although I met him only once, I must also express gratitude to the late L. Brent Bohlke, not only for his courtesy on that occasion, but also for his invaluable collection of interviews, speeches, and letters (*Willa Cather in Person*), which moves us so much closer to Cather the person. Without his research, part 2 of this study would offer a thinner view of Cather as author and as personality.

I also thank the staffs of the Newberry Library, Chicago; the Clifton Waller Barrett Library, the University of Virginia; and the Willa Cather Historical Center, Red Cloud, for their assistance.

I especially thank my colleague Tony Parise for reading early drafts of this study, and for urging always a straightforward clarity. I also thank two helpful English Department secretaries, Emilie Dahan and Marie Hall.

I am grateful to the officers of Grand Valley State University, Allendale, Michigan, for a sabbatical leave and one semester of reduced teaching that gave me valuable research time.

Gordon Weaver, the series editor, and Liz Traynor Fowler, of Twayne Publishers, have been helpful throughout.

Finally, I thank my husband, Irving Wasserman, for his unfailing encouragement.

Part 1

THE SHORT FICTION

Initial Bearings and
the Question of Modernism

To describe the working habits of Professor St. Peter, the writer-historian in her novel *The Professor's House*, Willa Cather drew on an extended simile: "Just as, when Queen Mathilde was doing the long tapestry now shown at Bayeux,—working her chronicle of the deeds of knights and heroes,—alongside the big pattern of dramatic action she and her women carried the little playful pattern of birds and beasts that are a story in themselves."[1] This fanciful image of parallel paths serves for Cather's own writing as well—her novels being "the big pattern" for which she is best known, and her short stories "the little playful pattern." The comparison holds if not pushed too far: Cather did indeed write short stories, some sixty of them, throughout her life (true, more earlier than later), and at times she was experimental in her short works—sketches, tales of the supernatural, fables, vignettes. Her best are not decorative birds and beasts, however; they are, like her novels, "chronicles" of her world. And they are indeed "a story in themselves."

That being so, it is puzzling that Cather's short fiction has not risen in popular and academic esteem along with her novels. A glance at any dozen well-known short story collections turns up only "Paul's Case," and that sporadically. Texts for American literature survey courses are more generous, usually including "Neighbour Rosicky" as well. If, as seems likely, interest in the stories is merely lagging behind critical consideration of the novels, anthologists will soon venture others—perhaps the delicate "Enchanted Bluff," or the equally subtle "Two Friends." Most deserving of all is "Old Mrs. Harris," perhaps Cather's greatest work in this genre. This story of three generations of women under one roof indeed throws "a luminous streak out into the shadowy realm of personal relationships," as Cather described the best of Katherine Mansfield's stories.[2]

In fairness, I must add that Cather herself made it difficult to encounter her short stories. A severe self-critic, she preferred to forget her early work, some of it written under the press of deadlines or the

3

need for money. She usually refused to allow republication in anthologies, except for "Paul's Case," which helps to explain its popularity, and she left copyright restrictions as to what stories could be reprinted. When she arranged for book publication she rejected many, pruned those she did select, and gave careful thought to sequence of subject and theme—care that extended to book design and typeface. Only three collections appeared in her lifetime. Clearly she thought of these books as more than simple collections and disliked having stories wrested from them.

For these reasons, and for others having to do with the vagaries of literary reputation, Cather's short stories have served only as dim background in the picture of Cather the writer.

Cather the writer—the phrase conjures up more than the works themselves. Increasingly, we seek the person behind the artist—mind, sensibility, life experiences—a chancy business at best, and doubly so for Cather, who gave careful thought to frustrating future biographers. She left no journals or diaries, no early drafts of her works remain for study, and she destroyed letters and asked correspondents to destroy those she had written to them. Still, memoirs and biographies have accumulated—finding questions, guessing at answers, filling out the picture. And the life touches the works in illuminating ways. The least confessional of writers, Cather nevertheless wrote from observation and experience. It is a rare Cather story whose locale is not a spot she knew firsthand, and intimately: a hallmark of her writing is its sure sense of place, of particular light or atmosphere. Former Nebraska neighbors entertained themselves with guessing which of them had gone into what characters. Further, Cather's beliefs—moral, aesthetic, even philosophic, though never held as a system—infuse her stories. What she thought about shapes her fiction.

We begin, then, with a glance at the woman Willa Cather, conscious, always, that the ill-marked path between the life and the writing runs two ways. The stories discussed here illumine the cast of the author's sensibility and vision even as the facts of her life provide a frame and context for her stance toward the world.

A Biographical Sketch

In her memoir of Cather, Elizabeth Shepley Sergeant, herself a writer and journalist, makes a striking statement: "Willa Cather stands out as closer than any other writer of stature I have known to living Goethe's dictum: We approach the world through art, and art is our link with it."[3] Sergeant's account of her long friendship with Cather, focusing on their endless talk about writing and authors, gives us the best picture we have of Cather in the years when she was turning from professional journalism to writing full-time. Biographers of the earlier years, of her girlhood and student days, and of her first efforts at writing, point in another direction—to dislocations and struggle rather than studious leisure; to the sharp pains of homesickness and to jobs with hard deadlines and demanding bosses.

Cather, the oldest of seven children, was born in rural Virginia, a descendant of families long settled there. When she was nine her father moved the family to Nebraska, still in the 1880s a raw land of red-grass plains and scattered railroad towns. In later life she described it as being "thrown out into a country as bare as a piece of sheet iron." Here lies the basis for both her love and her fear of the great plains, land and people—feelings that vibrate through so many of her stories. She never lost the shiver of dread she felt on that first bumpy wagon ride out to her grandfather's farm, when the immense land seemed to threaten "an erasure of personality."[4] Her first attempts at writing were sketches of lives on this land, and in the end she came to see beauty in its bleakness and drama in the pinched lives of the settlers and immigrants peopling the land around Red Cloud, the town whose wooden sidewalks and treeless streets appear in all her fictional small towns, whether placed in Nebraska, Kansas, or Colorado. Although as an adult she did not live on the plains that so filled her imagination, she never lost touch with family and friends in Red Cloud—even in the thirties, with her parents dead and brothers and sisters scattered, she sent gifts and cash to old friends hard pressed by depression and drought.

Cather's earliest ambition was to study medicine,[5] an interest lying behind her extraordinary high school graduation speech, in which she lectured the townspeople on the need for vivisection. The Red Cloud *Chief* noted laconically that "her line of thought was well carved out and a great surprise to her many friends."[6] Indeed it was thought out: she placed vivisection in the context of "all human history," terming it the latest battle in the long war against superstition, a mark of the human "exodus from barbarism." On one subject she is cautious: she does not mention Darwin, though she had been discussing evolution with Mr. Ducker, an Englishman regarded in the town as an eccentric dreamer (she always liked talking with older people). Cather read Latin and Greek with him, helped with scientific experiments in a little home laboratory, and, according to the memoir written by Edith Lewis, Cather's longtime companion and friend, "had long talks with him—about Christianity, about good and evil, about evolution."[7] Though she avoided this one topic, the voice is brash—it does not mind saying shocking things, and it loves the sound of words.

At sixteen, Cather enrolled in the University of Nebraska, first majoring in science, but soon, sometime in her second year, in literature. The move to Lincoln and to literary studies marks the second great displacement in her life, this a cultural one. Less abrupt than the move from Virginia to Nebraska, and less dramatic, it carried an anguish of its own—the painful fear of being already too far behind, of discovering intellectual gaps where others, accustomed to sophisticated families and foreign travel, moved with ease. In Lincoln, Cather became a friend of Louise Pound and the young Dorothy Canfield (later Fisher), both to become distinguished scholars and writers, and both from homes where learning was taken for granted. Cather's sense of inferiority rankled long. Sergeant states that Cather "could at any time feel impatient with the limits of her prairie education" (Sergeant, 65). Resentment can be detected in stories written some eight or ten years later—for example, in the 1902 story "Flavia and Her Artists," in which Cather modeled Flavia, a silly collector of "interesting" people, on Dorothy's mother, a notable art patron whose name was Flavia.[8]

Yet such inferiority as there was in Cather's prairie education she made up for with voracious reading, as the newspaper writing that she did while still a student makes abundantly clear. In her junior year Cather began to write theater and book reviews for the *Nebraska State Journal* and Lincoln *Courier*, launching a journalistic career that would last some twenty years. Her authoritative tone in these pieces (the voice had lost none of its brashness) was such that her opinion of actors and performances was dreaded by traveling companies more than the reviews in metropolitan papers ("that meatax young girl" her editor called her).[9] Indeed, to read the volumes of her collected early journalism is to be first amazed at the erudition, and finally, recalling her youth, amused—she handles classic and contemporary authors with equal aplomb, neatly pigeonholing as she goes, shifting without qualm from lavish praise to withering scorn. This pose of self-assurance, and the ease with which she alluded to all of literary and cultural history, made her a presence in Lincoln by the time she graduated in 1896. The story of her first meeting with Stephen Crane suggests the cost of all this work: Crane, on assignment in Nebraska for his newspaper syndicate, stopped at the office of the *Journal* after midnight and was startled to find a girl there asleep standing up (Lewis, 37).

Also while still a student, Cather began writing stories herself, short pieces about the people on the Divide, the ridge of hard land outside Red Cloud that defied all but the hardiest settlers. A suicide ("Peter"), an eccentric ("Lou, the Prophet"), a primitive wife abduction ("On the Divide"), these sketches testify to Cather's deep response to the land she had been thrust into, and to the lives it molded and distorted.

To learn about art and to create art oneself—these were exalting aspirations, and the young Cather wrote about the devotion they required in transcendent terms: "In the kingdom of art there is no God, but one God, and his service is so exacting that there are few men born of women who are strong enough to take the vows."[10] Together, these desires—to know all about "the kingdom of art" and to enter it herself as a writer—took hold of Cather, and never weakened their grasp.

The final major displacement of Cather's life came shortly after graduation with her move to the East, first to Pittsburgh for ten years, and then in 1906 to New York, which remained her home. She went to Pittsburgh to edit a small periodical aimed at domestic improvement, the *Home Monthly,* but soon moved to the more congenial atmosphere of the Pittsburgh *Daily Leader,* where she worked on the news desk and wrote theater and music criticism. Her friends were fellow journalists, actresses, and musicians, some of whom appear, transmuted, in stories she would write long after leaving Pittsburgh. In 1901 Cather began teaching high school, which she had turned to in an effort to find time for her own writing.

Her writing soon led to her move to New York. A sheaf of stories submitted to *McClure's* caught the attention of S. S. McClure himself, who impulsively offered Cather a position on the magazine and promised to publish her stories as a book. Present-day journalism offers no analog to *McClure's Magazine* and its adventurous editor: he and it were a force both for literature (he printed fiction and poetry by Kipling, Stevenson, Conrad, Henry James, Sarah Orne Jewett, and Housman) and for social reform (his muckraking writers—Ida Tarbell, Lincoln Steffans—were the most aggressive in the business).

Cather's career at *McClure's* was by all accounts a brilliant one. It began with long months researching the life of Mary Baker Eddy in Boston, where she met Sarah Orne Jewett, who quickly became a friend and mentor, and other figures in Boston cultural life. As an editor, and later managing editor, Cather went on manuscript hunts to London, where she met William Archer, the theater critic, who took her to see the Abbey players, seating her in Yeats's box, and who introduced her to H. G. Wells, Ford Maddox Hueffer (later Ford), and Lady Gregory. It was a life at the heart of things, heady, as her friend Edith Lewis wrote, "to one born on the far frontiers of the world, where only the faintest trickle comes through of the great traditions" (Lewis, 55). But it gave her little time for herself, and in 1912 she at last made up her mind to leave the magazine to try supporting herself by her writing. This she did, at first precariously, but as novel followed novel—*Alexander's Bridge, O Pioneers!, The Song of the Lark, My Ántonia*—with greater assurance. After she received the Pulitzer Prize of 1922 for *One of Ours*, Cather's position was secure, and her life took on a more leisurely aspect. She traveled—to Europe, to an island off New Brunswick where she built a summer cabin, to the Far West, and always back to Red Cloud for long visits. (Social historians of American railroading would do well to read Cather: lonely Western depots, swaying coaches, baggage cars, brakemen, telegraphers—all are there. One little tale of the supernatural, "The Affair at Grover Station," depends on detailed knowledge of freight scheduling.) But mostly she read and wrote, approaching life, as Sergeant noted, through art—books, painting, and music, especially opera and especially Wagner.

The coming of World War II oppressed her. She patiently answered the many letters from servicemen who wrote her, touched that they found her books comforting in faraway places. She died in 1947 and is buried in Jaffrey, New Hampshire, in a country graveyard near an inn that she liked.

The Question of Modernism

What was the nature of the art that was Cather's "link to the world"? Answers have varied, depending on where in the literary spectrum the critic places her work. Clearly the deepest layers of her consciousness were formed by the great nineteenth-century romantics: a yearning for an ineffable completeness pervades her writing, early and late, and her penchant for the strenuous in the late romanticism of Carlyle, Wagner, and Turner is well documented (Rosowski, Chapter 1 and passim). However, so protean is romanticism that to assert its primacy leads to other questions—most importantly, to how its assumptions entered the currents of intellectual life at the turn of the century, and how Cather responded. These are matters hard to pin down, but increasingly critics are asserting that after all Cather belongs in her own time, the twentieth century—that is, with the modernists.

This has not been a placement arrived at easily. By date of birth, 1873, she could fit with the precursors of modernism—Stephen Crane, for example, or Sherwood Anderson—and she wrote during the heyday of modernism itself. But her narrative style, only gently experimental, and her settings—the monotonous plains (not even the *real* West)—consigned her at first to the local colorists, or realists of the everyday. Katherine Anne Porter recalled that Cather's simplicity "finally alienated me from her, from her very fine books, from any feeling that she was a living working artist in our time."[11] Ezra Pound, writing about Frost in a review of *North of Boston*, neatly articulates the prejudice of the self-conscious modernists against anything smacking of the homespun: "A book about a dull, stupid, hemmed-in sort of life, by a person who has lived it, will never be as interesting as the work of some author who has comprehended many men's manners and seen many grades and conditions of existence."[12] With two counts against her, as it were, critics have only slowly perceived the modernist elements in her style and themes.

As it happens, Frost may serve as a doubly useful analogue. In a number of ways Cather and Frost suffered similar critical vicissitudes. They were born in the same decade, only one year apart (oddly, both gave for a time later birth dates). They knew each other's work. Cather "took him for her own at once," Sergeant says (Sergeant, 133). She felt that he, too, was "one of the roughs," that they shared a "passionate dependence on the world of nature," and that they both "liked a bare and timeless world" (Sergeant, 212). Both resented being classified as simple realists, portrayers of the countryside and rural folk. A better self-publicist than Cather, Frost lived to see the philosophical core of his work perceived; only in recent years have critics noted the similar underpinning of Cather's writing.

Cather's reputation, then, falls roughly into two periods. The first, that hers is a retrograde art, changes colors through several decades: first she was seen as a regionalist of the Hamlin Garland variety, a categorization Cather always found irksome; then, for a time in the thirties, when the proletarian novel was the standard, she was dismissed as a prettifier of life; that view shifted in the fifties toward toleration for her elegiac pictures of the pioneer past. Then a new critical view began to form, focusing first on elements of her style: structures taken from myth and folktale, networks of symbol and allusion, oral stories and tales, broken chronologies, images and motifs from painting and music—in short, the techniques of the early modernists.

Gradually, too, critics are finding that her themes and preoccupations are those of the early modernists. This latter point, so important for reading her stories, needs further elaboration. Modernism, like romanticism, is a constellation of many ideas, prejudices, and postures, not all of which Cather shared.

This is not the place to pursue the much-debated question of how modernism is to be understood, nor is there any need. Now that it has receded, its lineaments are apparent and generally agreed to: there was indeed a striking movement in all the arts in the first three decades of the twentieth century; it was international; it absorbed the latest in thought from anthropologists, linguists, and cosmologists; and it sought new forms of expression. Perhaps the weight of historical and cultural experience had reached a critical mass, demanding the breakup of old notions of sequence and logic. This challenge to old forms gave a revolutionary flavor to what was a loose movement. Certainly Cather was no part of a group, though she knew, for example, Frieda and D. H. Lawrence and admired his work ("Have you ever read *Sea and Sardinia?*" she asked Sergeant, "Lawrence there used the language of *cubisme*" [Sergeant, 200]). Sergeant tells us that she read widely among the modernists and made her judgments. She liked Virginia Woolf, who dealt with "the inner side of things," and she found *Ulysses* a "landmark." Her devotion to high culture might have recommended Eliot to her, but apparently she found him pretentious. Stein and Pound were too anarchic, and O'Neill too gloomy. Proust was an early favorite. Her essay on Katherine Mansfield's short stories comments on Mansfield's ability "to approach the major forces of life through comparatively trivial incidents," a description that encapsulates, as it were, the aesthetic of literary modernism (*OW* 94).

Sergeant could not persuade her to take Freud seriously, nor, later, Jung. But "though she rejected Freud, she was a reader of Henri Bergson" (Sergeant, 203). Bergson and to a somewhat lesser degree William James, his older American contemporary, are two of the thinkers central to forming the modernist sensibility, as studies of Eliot, Faulkner, and Frost—to confine examples to American authors—have abundantly shown.[13] Cather read James and Bergson as their works came out, as did everyone interested in ideas. A friend from her Pittsburgh days has written that Cather was then "a devoted disciple" of William James.[14] Her enthusiasm for Bergson came later. She would have heard his ideas discussed on her trips to London for *McClure's*, for Bergsonianism was then the topic of the day among artists and advanced thinkers. In 1912 Cather wrote to Sergeant praising Bergson's *Creative Evolution*, just then translated.[15] In 1922 she alludes to Bergson in asserting that a writer must depend not on conscious faculties only, but on "what Mr. Bergson calls the wisdom of intuition as opposed to intellect."[16]

An expanded view of the powers of mind was indeed what James and Bergson were developing. James wrote that it is "the reinstatement of the vague and inarticulate to its proper place in our mental life which I am so anxious to press on the attention."[17] Bergson similarly propounded an essential role for intuition in the economy of mind: linked to involuntary memory, intuition serves as a conduit not only into the personal past, but, mysteriously, into the heart of the universe, into the flow of energy (his famous phrase, the *élan vital*) uniting the physical and human worlds. Sergeant was right to juxtapose Freud and Bergson: Cather preferred the Bergsonian version of the protean power of unconscious memory—sensual, but not narrowly sexual, bringing comforts of a metaphysical nature.

Important for their contemporary fame, and for Cather's interest, was the welcoming stance James and Bergson gave to evolution. James's *Principles of Psychology* (1890) and the later *Psychology: Briefer Course*, widely used as a college text to introduce the new science of mind, were commissioned by Henry Holt for a science series to popularize evolution to an American audience. But the picture of evolution that emerges in James, and even more eloquently in Bergson's *Creative Evolution* of 1907 (its publication date in France) is not of imponderable material forces, of chance and mortal struggle, but of vital, dynamic change driven by mind, or spirit. The universe is not closed, bound by iron determinacies, but open and free, still being made. Connected to this evolving world, the individual consciousness does not feel isolated, or overwhelmed, as in a novel by Hardy, but enhanced and made whole.

Bergson's theory of the twofold aspect of memory (voluntary recall, which orients us in practical and scientific matters, and involuntary surges of personal memory and insight) is related to his ideas about the dual nature of time, for which he is best known today. Clock time, or chronological time, is a series of measured, separate units—time spatialized, or geometrized. Necessary for daily life and for science, it is essentially artificial. The other time, Bergson's *durée* (duration), is experienced, or lived time, felt in the ceaseless flow of qualitative change—layered, simultaneous moments that interpenetrate the present. (To offer one example of these ideas fictionalized: in "The Bookkeeper's Wife," a slight sketch Cather wrote in 1916 about a life entirely crushed under the weight of chronological time, Bixby, the bookkeeper, spends his life working to pay for his wife's furniture, including a Mission clock "as big as a coffin and with nothing but two weights dangling in its hollow framework.")[18]

This core of ideas about the nature of consciousness, time, and memory entered the ground of Cather's thinking during the early years of her serious writing, reorienting her early romanticism. Indeed, the ideas of James and Bergson may be interpreted as validating many insights of the great romantics. Bergson's intuition resembles Coleridge's shaping power of imagination, and Woolf's "moments of being" or Joyce's "epiphanies" seem very like Wordsworth's "spots of time"— sudden and evanescent insights into a central meaning. But James and Bergson did more than give a new spin to old ideas: with their grounding in science (Bergson was trained as a biologist and James in medicine), they gave the generation coming of age in the early years of this century—the modernists—confidence to confront the scientism and pessimism of the late nineteenth century. Evolutionary vitalism underlies many Cather stories.

Cather's Aesthetic

Despite an early enthusiasm for Poe and his theory of the short story ("Poe found short story writing a bungling makeshift. He left it a perfect art. . . . He first gave the short story purpose, method, and artistic form"),[19] Cather did not really bother about careful definitions. Some of her own stories are novella length ("Coming, Aphrodite!" and "Uncle Valentine"), almost as long as *My Mortal Enemy*, which is considered a novel. At least two novels began as short stories: *O Pioneers!* was first two stories, "The White Mulberry Tree" and "Alexandra," and the middle section of *The Professor's House*, called "Tom Outland's Story" in the novel, in fact has been published separately as a story, "The Blue Mesa." It seems clear that when ideas or subjects occurred to Cather she let them seek their own length and form. This notion is borne out by her comments on how she composed.

It is important to note that when Cather wrote or spoke about writing as a technique, her references, always to "the novel," apply equally to narrative in general. She did not write much: her views appear in a few brief essays, a few discussions of the writing of others, and, in the early years, some interviews and speeches. In all of these she stresses the same points—brevity, concentration, concern for a hard-to-define authenticity. In her best-known essay, "The Novel Démeublé," she argues for an austere selectivity of detail, for "unfurnishing" the social-historical surroundings and even the moods and emotions of characters (she thinks D. H. Lawrence overdoes the data of emotions). The notion of art as selection is hardly a new one; Cather appears to be reacting against the school of everyday realism. Of greater interest is her second point, that the true subject does not appear on the page; rather, it inheres in the "inexplicable presence of the thing not named."[20] She points out that the true work of the "furniture" is to convey something about figures in the story, not to lend verisimilitude to a scene: Tolstoy's interiors "seem to exist, not so much in the author's mind, as in the emotional penumbra of the characters themselves" (*OW*, 40).

In a speech given in 1925 Cather speaks of the "spiritual" plot inside the "crude" or "coarse" plot,[21] and of the moment when emotion "flares up"—the end toward which everything has been converging, which may not be the actual conclusion. Stories of great love, she says, are successful only "when they flame up as volcanic fires through the crust."[22] Here the "flaring up" imagery inescapably reminds us of Joyce's epiphany: perhaps they were both thinking of the same tongues of flame.

Cather's comments on the artistic process itself, on how writers "get ideas" for stories, stress the inexplicable: A writer must depend on Bergsonian intuition. Only young writers have specific opinions that they want to defend; serious writers must let something that "teases the mind for years" finally find its form (Sergeant, 107). The beginning of a story lies in "a personal explosional experience" that is allowed to wait until "the form fixes itself." Hence experimentation must be expected: "The arts cannot stand still; if they mark time, they die. There must be experimenting, if that is the right word for it."[23]

Cather's aesthetic accords well with the modern short story as it has come to be defined. The "epiphanic moment," the moment of illumination so labeled and exemplified by Joyce, has been widely accepted as the hallmark of the modernist short story emerging from the traditional tale and the realistic sketch. (I leave untouched the question of whether such a moment of coming together cannot be discerned in the stories of earlier writers like Hawthorne.) Oft-repeated definitions stress, too, that the epiphany strikes, or arises from, the ordinary events of the story—for example, Hortense Calisher's "An Apocalypse, served in a very small cup."

It remains to place Cather's stories against these tenets of modernism, to see whether, in the main, her work is clarified and enhanced by that frame. Two stories from different periods will serve as test cases. Cather was still at *McClure's* when she wrote "The Enchanted Bluff"; she completed "Before Breakfast" in the late forties, only shortly before she died.

The Modern Short Story: Two Examples

"The Enchanted Bluff."   In her memoir, Edith Lewis recalls that during the *McClure's* years Cather was not satisfied with the stories she was trying to write, with one exception—"The Enchanted Bluff." Lewis writes, "It was as if she had here stopped trying to make a story, and had let it make itself, out of instinctive memories, deep-rooted forgotten things" (Lewis, 70).

The setting is a sandbar in a western river very like the Republican River as it runs just outside Red Cloud, a favorite haunt of the Cather children and their friends on hot summer days. A group of six adolescent boys—one has finished high school, another is older still—build a campfire on the sandbar and spend the night. Gradually their idle talk focuses on one boy's dream of someday journeying to New Mexico and scaling the Enchanted Bluff, a mesa that no one has visited since an ancient people, cliff dwellers, perished there, marooned by storm and accident. The boys vow that whoever gets there first must tell the others, and with that promise they sleep, happily ignorant of what will be their true destinies, told in a coda by the now grown-up narrator.

The story quickly individualizes the boys. Fritz and Otto Hassler, sons of the German tailor in Sandtown, earn money selling catfish; they are "as brown and sandy as the river itself."[24] Percy Pound spends his high school days reading detective stories behind his desk; that night on the river the other boys try again, futilely, to show Percy the Little Dipper. The oldest boy, Arthur Adams, has "fine hazel eyes that were almost too reflective and sympathetic for a boy," but a habit of idleness, of "lounging with a lot of us little fellows," has set him on the path that will lead to a seat under a cottonwood behind one of the town's saloons (*CSF*, 71). Tip Smith works in his father's grocery store every afternoon and mornings before school. Even so, he spends hours with a little scroll saw. He values relics that a Baptist missionary peddled to his father, "seeming to derive satisfaction from their remote origin" (*CSF*, 71). The devotion to design and the fascination with an exotic past are significant traits, and it is Tip who tells the legend of the Enchanted Bluff. A sixth boy, never named, narrates the story. He has finished high school and is about to begin teaching school out on the Divide (as did one of Cather's brothers), "a windy plain that was all windmills and corn fields and big pastures; where there was nothing wilful or unmanageable in the landscape, no new islands, and no chance of unfamiliar birds—such as often followed the watercourses" (*CSF*, 70).

The river, always changing, dominates the story. It is an image for the evolving natural world, ever building, providing tenuous "homes"—the sandbars that are "a little new bit of world" (*CSF*, 70):

> The channel was never the same for two successive seasons. Every spring the swollen stream undermined a bluff to the east, or bit out a few acres of corn field somewhere else. When the water fell low in midsummer, new sand bars were thus exposed to dry and whiten in the August sun. Sometimes these were banked so firmly that the fury of the next freshet failed to unseat them; the little willow seedlings emerged triumphantly . . . and with their mesh of roots bound together the moist sand. (*CSF*, 69–70)

The river, too, dominates the talk of the boys: As they lie back under the stars, under the "dark cover of the world" (*CSF*, 72), they begin to speak of distant times and places. "My father says that there was another North Star once, and that maybe this one won't last always," Otto asserts (*CSF*, 72). The moon rising over the river bluffs, "an enormous, barbaric thing, red as an angry heathen god" (*CSF*, 72), makes Percy think of Aztec human sacrifices, which Arthur confirms ("The moon was one of their gods" [*CSF*, 72]). The current over a log boils up "like gold pieces," and Fritz wonders about the gold hidden in the river, gold that, Arthur says, Coronado and his men came to hunt for. "The Spaniards came all over this country once." "Before the Mormons went through?" says dull-witted Percy. "Before the Pilgrim Fathers, Perce," he is told (*CSF*, 73). Inspired by the river, its vitality, its renewing force, the boys have peopled their universe with the remotest past of the great continent—not a thin veneer of civilization, but a rich, many-layered simultaneity of past lives and forms.

Then Tip tells about the Enchanted Bluff, a story his Uncle Bill, "a wanderer, bitten with mining fever," had told him (*CSF*, 74). Tip's account of the lost civilization takes the boys to an unspecifiable time "before the Spaniards came," far to the West where "there aren't no railroads or anything" (*CSF*, 74). Someday, somehow, Tip will reach the top. What will he find? Fritz asks. "Bones, maybe, or the ruins of their town, or pottery, or some of their idols. There might be 'most anything up there. Anyhow, I want to see." And so do they all—to journey, to see.

Suddenly the narrator, grown up, tells us that no one made the journey. He has gone to college and returns to Sandtown only on visits. On one he sees Arthur, who even in the saloon backyard (where later he will die) recalls "Tip Smith's Bluff." Percy is a stockbroker in Kansas City and obsessed with motor cars. The Hassler boys and Tip himself never leave Sandtown, but Tip still talks of going to New Mexico, and now he plans to take his boy Bert with him, who, the last line of the story tells us, "has been let in on the story, and thinks of nothing but the Enchanted Bluff."

Without violating the surface naturalism of her story, Cather transfigures a memory from her childhood into a meditation on the human condition. Through the boys' talk, moving by fits and starts, by association, and through impressionistic glimpses of the river, the sand, the night, the reader is led to see the little group enveloped and enmeshed in a vibrant cosmos, just as the little willow roots enmesh the sand. The night sky is "the dark cover of the world," and past time (the Mormon trek, Coronado's explorations, the Aztec sacrifices, the ancient people of the mesa) joins dreams of possibility, both near ("we could embark at Sandtown in floodtime, follow our noses, and eventually arrive at New Orleans" [*CSF*, 73] and distant (climbing the mesa). Inspired by the river and the night sky, as was the young Wordsworth by the lake at Grasmere, the boys imaginatively move through the logic of dream and association to feel the unity of the natural and human worlds.

But the ending is sad: forgetting (Percy's obsession with motor cars), early death (Arthur), accident (Fritz loses his foot working on the railroad), vain hope (Tip's deflection of the dream to his son, Bert), and disillusion (the narrator now calls "the Project" only "the romance of the lone red rock"). The sadness shocks the reader—a moment of illumination—into realizing the darker implications of the boys' talk. Unlike the young Wordsworth, who absorbed serenity and reassurance from surrounding nature, the Sandtown boys sense instability—a post-Darwinian universe of cruel superstition, extinct peoples, stars that may shift or burn out. The river speaks with two voices: "Our water had always these two moods: the one of sunny complaisance, the other of inconsolable, passionate regret" (*CSF, 72*). The river speaks of the precariousness and transience of existence: not only is the river subject to change; the bluff itself was brought by a glacier, and its base is worn by wind and sand. Only the "enchantment" survives—the "romance" held in the human imagination and perpetuated by story, from Uncle Bill to Tip to Tip's son. The themes are romantic (the link to the natural world, the power of imagination) but also Bergsonian (the world in process, the *élan vital* surging through both physical and human forms). While not sunny, this insight mitigates the regret voiced so passionately by the river.

Like Virginia Woolf's lighthouse, the bluff, an ultimate destination promising fulfillment, is never to be reached. Nevertheless, both give meaning and direction across the gulfs of time, though what that meaning is must remain ineffable: both lighthouse and bluff are in the real world, built by man or touched by him (the lost civilization), inevitably subject to change, their meaning an endowment of human imagination.

Cather had written an earlier story, "The Treasure of Far Island," about children playing on a river sandbar. She encumbers it with a grown-up love affair and many allusions to *Treasure Island*. To compare the two is to see what Cather meant by throwing out the furniture.

"Before Breakfast." A similar insight into the essential unity of the physical and human worlds informs "Before Breakfast," one of the last stories Cather finished. The setting is an island in the North Atlantic off the coast of Nova Scotia—in fact, a large rock brought there by a glacier, like the New Mexico mesa. How to think about the rock is the question of the story.

The island, with its cool dark spruces and high cliffs, is modeled after Grand Manan, where Cather had a summer home. She loved its remoteness and quiet, feelings she gives to Henry Grenfell, the businessman who is the central figure of the story—indeed, the only one; others enter only through his memories and thoughts.

Fatigued by business and family affairs, Grenfell has come to the island for a rest, and the story covers the first morning of his solitary vacation. Grenfell has passed a sleepless night, disturbed initially by thinking of an annoying geologist he had encountered on the boat train. The scientist had insisted on speaking of statistics: the island is 136 million years old, pushed here by a glacier, and, oddly, the two ends of the island are from two different periods. "And about how old would our end be, Professor?" Grenfell had asked, feigning indifference, but giving himself away by the possessive pronoun.[25] Now, in the morning, he remembers again, resentfully, the loss of his private ownership to the indifferent ages. How like a scientist, he thinks, not to have a real home on the island, but instead a "portable house" (his tent) that he will take up next year and move to some island in the South Pacific. Only the professor's attractive daughter, who seemed to sense Grenfell's love of the island as a refuge, had relieved the trip.

Grenfell's sleepless night has led to other revelations about sources of irritation in his life, and to a picture of his past. His life has been all struggle, though successful struggle, from the age of thirteen, when he quit school to help his family, through reading law late at night, to his own bond business in New York and to a marriage that has "worked out as well as most" (*OBO*, 151) and that has given him three sons, now grown. The cost of his success is high: only with difficulty can he quell his "hair-trigger stomach." At times he eats like an anchorite, on graham crackers and milk. He finds some relief in long annual hunting trips for North American big game, taking satisfaction in convincing the guides that he is not just a delicate dyspeptic. His doctors tell him that he takes everything too hard. "Apparently it was not the brain that desired and achieved," he thought, but something more primitive: "Perhaps he was a throw-back to the Year One, when in the stomach was the only constant, never sleeping, never quite satisfied desire" (*OBO*, 157).

Grenfell's memories during the night suggest a man fiercely independent and private, who has attacked life with will and intellect alone. Just the day before, he "triumphed" over his son Harrison, who had asked where his father would be staying and for how long. Grenfell cut him off by stating that his secretary had all the necessary information. Then, when Harrison picked up a book that his father was packing (*Henry IV, Part One*, about a king who finds ruling a burden, whose only comfort is reconciliation with his son), Grenfell cuts off his interest. Perhaps, he reflects, he had been too short, but then, his son "had no business to touch anything in his father's bag" (*OBO*, 154). Grenfell "resented any intrusion on his private, personal non-family life."

As the night wore on, Grenfell felt "everything that was shut up in him, under lock and bolt and pressure . . . spread out into the spaciousness of the night, undraped, unashamed" (*OBO*, 149–50). It had been "one of those nights of revelation, revaluation, when everything seems to come clear . . . only to fade out again in the morning" (*OBO*, 149).

Grenfell prepares for his morning walk by getting out eye drops (a scientific aid to clarity), but stops suddenly at the sight of the low-hung morning star, Venus, "serene, impersonal splendour" older even than 136 million years (*OBO*, 144). Grenfell salutes her as an ally: "And what's a hundred and thirty-six million years to you, Madam? . . . the rocks can't tell any tales on you. You were doing your stunt up there long before there was anything down here but—God knows what!" Thus reassured of a mystery in the universe unsolved by "professors" (and without eye drops), Grenfell sets out to reclaim "his" island.

On his walk, Grenfell gradually feels better; he sees white mushrooms lifting a heavy thatch of pine needles, and salutes the dead branches of a huge spruce that has weathered another year. Reaching a rocky headland, he sits down, feeling, he tells himself, like Pilgrim, who has left his burden at the bottom of the hill. Then occurs the one "incident" of this slim story. Down below in the surf, the geologist's daughter prepares to swim in the chill Atlantic. From a distance, the figure in the pink bathing suit emerging from her robe, "a grey thing lined in white," becomes both sea creature and myth—Venus rising from the waves. "If a clam stood upright and graciously opened its shell, it would look like that" (*OBO*, 164). Irrationally, for a moment, Grenfell thinks he should descend to rescue the girl. When he sees her resolutely face the cold water and successfully complete her swim, he is able to laugh at himself, but also, with a feeling of uplift, to participate in her youth and vitality.

The resolution is Bergsonian. Countering the cold, heavy weight of scientific time—the glacier, the eons of time—is the force, the energy, flowing through both matter and spirit: Venus (star, girl, and myth), the evolving sea creature, the story of Pilgrim seeking perfection, the girl's courage. Grenfell returns to his cottage meditating on the mysterious continuity of creative energy still moving through evolution: "Anyhow, when that first amphibious frog-toad found his water-hole

19

dried up, and jumped out to hop along till he could find another—well, he started on a long trip" (166). Grenfell's thoughts are expressed discursively by Bergson in *Creative Evolution:* "by the sympathetic communication which it establishes between us and the rest of the living, intuition introduces us into life's own domain, which is reciprocal interpenetration, endlessly continued creation."[26]

But has Grenfell read his two encounters with Venus fully? Could a design not yet apparent to him be at work? Grenfell's wakeful night revealed a man who "had got ahead wonderfully . . . but, somehow, ahead on the wrong road" (*OBO*, 158). What the reader perceives, and Grenfell cannot admit, is that he stands in need of the emanations from Venus not for intellectual reassurance only, but for emotional healing, for guidance in accepting the love and family affections he so successfully resists. (In the middle of his black night he momentarily saw this: "The bitter truth was that his worst enemy was closer even than the wife of his bosom—was his bosom itself!" [*OBO*, 156]).

There is something of John Marcher in Grenfell—the same obstinate fidelity to an obscure desire for fulfillment and the same blindness to the figure in the carpet that is pointing the way he should go. Whereas James's story ends with Marcher's shattering realization of what he has lost, Cather's avoids closure. Perhaps, after his epiphanic insight into the unchanging laws that govern the universe, after having responded to one lesson from Venus, Grenfell will be able to receive the overtures of his family (there is some evidence that his wife Margaret, like Harrison, has been more forebearing than Grenfell thinks). Perhaps he will avoid Marcher's awful fate.

In this small sketch, then, Cather tells two stories. The account of the objective present (Grenfell's morning) is juxtaposed to the subjective, unresolved past, both stories concerned to reveal a state of affairs to human consciousness—both unraveling the modern plot of revelation.

Like "The Enchanted Bluff," "Before Breakfast" ends without concluding: the perspective is vast (glaciers, stars, the impossibility of possessing even so solid a thing as an island of rock). Such a cosmos *may* be speaking to human understanding, but even if it is, we may not hear all that it is saying. Both stories are thoroughly in the modern idiom: condensed, allusive, suggesting the larger structures of existence beneath trivial incident.

Two Early Collections

The Troll Garden

The Troll Garden, Cather's first book of stories, came out in 1905, just before Cather joined the *McClure's* staff. The stories were all recent, written while Cather was teaching in Pittsburgh. Varied and uneven though they are, a common thread runs through all seven: in each, the central situation has to do with the nature of art and the artist's relation to life—problems of definition, of talent, of deluded self-perception, of sacrifices demanded, and rewards. Although the fictional artists are either sculptors, painters, and musicians or patrons of these arts, rather than writers (the sole exception is the devious M. Roux in "Flavia and Her Artists"), the young Cather, barely thirty, is no doubt writing from a personal concern, questioning the nature of this priestly kingdom that demands so much of its votaries. Her subject, the preeminent subject for modernism, is art itself, and the problem of understanding its place in the objective world.

The title of the collection refers to the book's epigraph, drawn from Charles Kingsley: "A fairy palace, with a fairy garden . . . Inside the Trolls dwell, . . . working at their magic forges, making and making always things rare and strange." The first edition carried as well a second epigraph from Christina Rosetti's poem "The Goblin Market," four lines beginning "We must not look at Goblin men, / We must not buy their fruits." Critics have explored the possible significances of these two excerpts, some searching the imagery for clues to Cather's subconscious sexual fears or longings.[27] However that may be, what is clear is that Cather is thinking of art as a world unlike any other, a world apart, a place of magic—and not all white magic. She strikes this note of menace again in the title of her second collection, *Youth and the Bright Medusa*, published seventeen years later, in which art presents a face that turns its followers to stone. Trolls, goblins, and the stony-hearted are not comfortable companions: what art demands of life was a question that worried Cather all her life.

"Paul's Case," the best known of the *Troll Garden* stories, and deservedly so, is the only story set in Pittsburgh, where Cather was writ-

21

ing, and its scenes have the immediacy of observed experience: a high school faculty meeting, the stoops of row houses on a Sunday afternoon, Carnegie Music Hall. Years later Cather stated that Paul had been composed from two memories, one of a nervous boy in her Latin class who claimed friendships with actors in the local stock company, and the other her own feelings on first seeing New York and the old Waldorf-Astoria Hotel.[28]

The story falls into two parts. In the first Paul is facing expulsion from high school for what seem minor kinds of insubordination and disrespect, the underlying cause being his exasperating contempt (as the teachers see it) toward the whole educational enterprise. In the opening scene he is called before a disciplinary committee to explain himself. The teachers are not unkind, but Paul's insouciant air (he enters "suave and smiling" with a red carnation in his buttonhole) both baffles and angers them. At the end of the hearing, they leave feeling "dissatisfied and unhappy; humiliated to have felt so vindictive toward a mere boy."[29] Paul rushes off to his ushering job at Carnegie Hall, first going up to the picture gallery in the Hall, where "he sat down before a blue Rico and lost himself" (*TG*, 104). Later, after helping patrons to their seats, he falls into a similar dreamy state as the symphony begins ("he lost himself as he had before the Rico" [105]).

The concert over, Paul delays long enough to follow the singer's carriage and watch her enter her hotel: "he seemed to feel himself go after her up the steps, into the warm, lighted building, into an exotic, a tropical world of shiny, glistening surfaces and basking ease" (107). A gust of cold wind and rain in his face rouses him, and he takes the cars to Cordelia Street, "where all the houses were exactly alike" (107). He pictures to himself his upstairs room, with its "horrible yellow wallpaper, . . . and over his painted wooden bed the pictures of George Washington and John Calvin, and the framed motto 'Feed My Lambs,' which had been worked in red worsted by his mother" (107). His father, with his endless questions and complaints, will be standing at the top of the stairs. (Paul's mother died when he was a baby, and Paul lives with his father and sisters, shadowy girls who barely appear in the story.)

When the school principal reports that Paul has not improved following the faculty hearing, Paul's father takes him out of school and finds a place for him as a cash boy with Denny & Carson—the first step, as Cordelia Street sees it, to a solid future. Further, Paul is required to quit ushering, and the doorkeeper is to see that he does not enter the theater. The second half of the story begins with Paul on a train to New York. On arrival he takes a cab to an expensive men's furnishing establishment, where he outfits himself with street and dress clothes, then to Tiffany's for a scarfpin and silver articles, and last to a trunk shop where his purchases are put in traveling bags. He registers at the Waldorf for a sleeping room, sitting room, and bath. In a brief flashback we learn that Paul has quietly stolen almost a thousand dollars in cash from Denny & Carson. It had been "astonishingly easy," and now Paul looks ahead with relief to a few "precious days" of ease: "This time there would be no awakening, no figure at the top of the stairs" (115). He luxuriates in his surroundings—the lavishly furnished hotel, hothouse flowers, the music in the dining room, and the city itself, including a night out with a freshman from Yale and an evening in a loge at the Metropolitan: "Everything was quite perfect; he was exactly the kind of boy he had always wanted to be" (115). On the eighth day he learns from the Pittsburgh papers that his theft has been discovered, and that his father is in New York looking for him: "It was to be worse than jail, even; the tepid waters of Cordelia Street were to close over him finally and forever. The grey monotony stretched before him in hopeless, unrelieved years; Sabbath-school, Young People's Meeting, the yellow-papered room, the damp dish-towels" (118). He enjoys one last evening in the hotel dining room, drinking more wine than usual, drumming nervously to the *Pagliacci* music in the background—a sound track signaling the inevitable tragedy and also the sad clownishness of the deluded boy in his masquerade. (Revising the story, Cather cut the reference to *Pagliacci*, possibly to remove the suggestion that Paul's true self was hidden, rather than revealed, by his new clothes.)[30] The next day Paul takes the ferry to New Jersey, then hires a horse cab to drive him into the countryside by the railroad track, where he dismisses the cab, walks to a high bank, and launches himself before an oncoming train. Before he jumps he takes one of the red flowers he has been wearing in his coat and buries it in the snow.

Critics generally follow the lead of Cather's title, which seems to hint that this is a "case study," a sociological or clinical examination of a completed, enclosed incident or pathological state. The most frequent reading sees a sensitive, artistically inclined youth crushed by a withering environment, the dreary rigidities of Pittsburgh Presbyterianism and the physical ugliness of Paul's home ("the cold bathroom with the grimy zinc tub, the cracked mirror, the dripping spiggots"

[107]). Adherents to this view in its most extreme form hold that in this story "environment is consistently portrayed as the inexhaustible determiner of human lives."[31] The two faces over his bed, Washington and Calvin, represent the failures of state (high school) and church.

Countering interpretations point out that Paul gives no evidence of suppressed talent or even fine-grained love of art; in fact, he appears to use art only as a vehicle for escapist dreams. Paul himself is the "case," and the story poses a psychological question: what is the etiology of such maladjustment? Early deprivation, the loss of his mother, is one explanation ("he could not remember the time when he had not been dreading something. Even when he was a little boy, it was always there—behind him or before, or on either side" [114]). The motto embroidered by his mother, "Feed My Lambs," symbolizes his poignant longing for love, a need not met by his father, a figure of judgment and punishment. In accord with this view of Paul as emotionally infantile, Cordelia Street is interpreted as an ordinary working-class community, full of children and plans for the future, its dreariness and ugliness a reflection of Paul's distorting vision. Possibly an older psychology, one less attuned to the importance of early childhood experiences, is behind Cather's portrait. Reading William James, Cather would have come across his discussion of types of "diseased will," including cases marked by an inability to plan or act. She would have been particularly sensitive to his speculation that too much theatergoing, or too much music listening, has a debilitating effect on forming constructive life habits (James, especially chapters 1, "Habit," and 17, "Will").

That "Paul's Case" responds to such contrasting readings is sufficient evidence that Cather succeeded in balancing the competing claims of the old arguments between nature and nurture, heredity and environment, freedom and determinism, and that the beauty of the story inheres in just this tension. Reflecting on the story, readers must reluctantly side with Paul's teachers (voices for the best understanding his culture could provide), admitting, as each does, "that it was scarcely possible to put into words the real cause of the trouble" (102).

More remains to be said. Accomplished as the whole story is, its real glory lies in the second half—the realization of the dream. Here is the source of the fascination the story continues to exert on the young and the not-so-young: to win without desert or guilt, to be queen-for-a-day, to be the lost heir. Against all odds, this wish is indeed fulfilled in the story, however temporarily. All the little failures that could have spoiled

Paul's week are avoided. He *does* know what he wants, and he enjoys fully the feel of his clothes, the white linen, the flowers blooming under glass, the red velvet carpets, the sound of popping corks. He is not embarrassed or gauche, as an uneducated, callow boy might be in such surroundings ("he wore his spoils with dignity and in no way made himself conspicuous. . . . His chief greediness lay in his ears and eyes, and his excesses were not offensive ones" [117]). The experienced clerks at the Waldorf take him at his own estimation; apparently he could spend an evening with a college boy without betraying his ignorance. Most intriguing of all is his mental poise ("He was not the least abashed or lonely. . . . He could not remember a time when he had felt so at peace with himself" [117]). No qualms about his crime disturb him; apparently the long lessons of Sabbath School gained no niche in his consciousness—in fact, he feels virtuous ("The mere release from the necessity of petty lying, lying every day and every day, restored his self-respect. . . . He felt a good deal more manly, more honest, even" [117]). Later, facing death, he still "had a feeling that he had made the best of it" (119). What he believes now with even greater certainty is "that money was everything" (119).

In giving Paul this irreverent final thought, Cather is doubtless playing with discreet irony against the sentimental moralists of her day, who would have anticipated a wave of guilt and remorse (in this regard, at least, she is like her admired Mark Twain). That this is her intent is underscored when Paul, falling before the train, sees "the folly of his haste . . . with merciless clarity"; but the "folly" is not his crime, not his suicide, not his false moral sense; rather, it is his failure to escape further, to more distant lands, to "the blue of Adriatic water, the yellow of Algerian sands" (121).

Modern psychologists say that we excuse, even find amusing, the extreme narcissists, who can take and enjoy without conscience (comic figures like Falstaff; great criminals), because deep down we understand these longings embedded in us from early infancy. Cather evokes these long-suppressed desires, and we accept as humanly right the forgiveness implicit in the delicate compassion of the lines ending Paul's story (not really a "case" at all): "Then, because the picture making mechanism was crushed, the disturbing visions flashed into black, and Paul dropped back into the immense design of things" (121).

Among the many delicate touches in the narration of Paul's story are a few hints that his apparent self-destructiveness is rather his fidelity to some dimly felt ultimacy, the "immense design of things." When

Paul is forced to give up the theater, Charley Edwards, the stock company juvenile, feels sorry because "he recognized in Paul something akin to what churchmen term 'vocation'" (110). An odd term, *vocation,* for the boy's obsession. The suggestion of a religious votive appears also as the narrator describes the childish dream of escape to another world that Paul builds to comfort himself through school and work. "So, in the midst of that smoke-palled city, enamoured of figures and grimy toil, Paul had his secret temple, his wishing carpet, his bit of blue-and-white Mediterranean shore bathed in perpetual sunshine" (111). The vision of sand and blue water that blesses Paul's final hour is the "secret temple" that has sustained him, and to which, in his fashion, he has been faithful.

Although a lesser story entirely, "The Garden Lodge," the third story of *The Troll Garden,* offers an interesting contrast to "Paul's Case." The "case" of Caroline Noble reports what may happen when conditions are reversed, when a child grows up in a household rich in artistic aspiration: "Ever since Caroline could remember, the law in the house had been a sort of mystic worship of things distant, intangible and unattainable . . . in talk of masters and masterpieces" (48). But the devotion to higher things on the part of her composer father, painter brother, and the mother who serves both entails not only nagging poverty ("boiled mutton and the necessity of turning the dining-room carpet") but demeaning humiliation (living in "cowardly fear of the little grocer on the corner" [48]).

Cather's irony is heavy: the father and brother are deluded, egoistic misfits: the father keeps his students waiting while he discusses "Schopenhauer with some bearded socialist"; her brother sleeps late, then wanders about the house, "a Turkish cap on his head and a cigarette hanging from between his long, tremulous fingers" (48). Caroline thinks only of escape, but where Paul drifts and dreams, Caroline plans and works. After her first modest success as a piano instructor, "she never permitted herself to look further than a step ahead, and set herself with all the strength of her will to see things as they are and meet them squarely" (49). Her final escape comes with marriage to Howard Noble, a widower and "a power on Wall Street" (49). At the time of the story, Caroline is a highly regarded, efficient patron, no longer one of art's victims. In that role she entertains at her home a famous tenor on tour. Playing accompaniment as d'Esquerré practices Siegfried's arias in her garden lodge, Caroline slowly, unconsciously, feels long-buried, never-acknowledged desires growing in her for something other than this "happy, useful, well-ordered life" (55). She is haunted by a buried self in the form of "an imploring little girlish ghost . . . wringing its hands and entreating for an hour of life" (54). In the end, d'Esquerré is gone and Caroline has regained her usual control, agreeing with her husband that the garden lodge should be pulled down and replaced by a more modern structure.

Different though they are, both "Paul's Case" and "The Garden Lodge," while acknowledging the superficialities that may attend a devotion to art, assert art's primacy: it is no less than life giving. Behind the tinsel and falseness of Paul's art and behind the disorder and pretensions of Caroline's family lies an undeniable reality—sustaining, the source of vital desire and meaning.

The satiric thrust of "The Garden Lodge" is more marked in "Flavia and Her Artists," the lead story of *The Troll Garden*, but in this story the object of ridicule is a group of artists who have achieved a modicum of fame rather than the would-be artists of Bohemia. They have been gathered by Flavia Hamilton at her Hudson River summer home—a pianist, a tenor, a Russian chemist, a professor "who has dug up Assyria," an advanced German woman (8). As a story, "Flavia and Her Artists" is too complicated for summary, and ultimately not very successful. What is notable is that the "villain," who publishes a scurrilous piece on his hostess, an act of the basest ingratitude, is "the best" artist (Flavia's favorite category)—M. Roux, the French novelist whose fame is secure. And the man who counters the insult in a selfless effort to protect Flavia is Arthur Hamilton, Flavia's businessman husband. What makes for excellence in the artist is in this story neatly sliced away from what makes for human excellence. "Flavia and Her Artists," along with the even more convoluted "The Marriage of Phaedra," is frequently termed Jamesian (Cather unfailingly acknowledged Henry James a master craftsman). Undeniably, both stories introduce a number of psychological crosscurrents—so many that the reader wearies of following them. Cather was right in never reprinting either.

Only two stories in *The Troll Garden* depend on Western settings or images of life on the prairies, but these—"The Sculptor's Funeral" and "A Wagner Matinee"—can rank with "Paul's Case" as among Cather's best. (Another, "'A Death in the Desert,'" is also set in the West, but it offers almost no glimpses of landscape or Western life, and indeed its major setting, a sickroom, borders on the claustrophobic.)

Had "The Sculptor's Funeral" been her only Western story, Cather could rightly be listed as a writer in the revolt-from-the-village tradition of Garland and Lewis. The inhabitants of the Kansas town who receive Harvey Merrick's body for burial are, with one exception, vulgar, grasping, and mean spirited. The exception is Jim Laird, Merrick's boyhood friend, now the town lawyer, an alcoholic filled with self-hatred for what the town has done to him. Laird has comforted himself with thinking of his friend's escape from "this place of hatred and bitter waters, . . . of him living off there in the world, away from this hog wallow" (44). Now early death has cut short Merrick's career, one marked by foreign awards, financial success, an adoring student.

This student, young Steavens, has accompanied his master's body from Boston back home, and through his eyes we are led to discover a deeper truth—that Merrick had never truly escaped, that he had never rid himself of the scars inflicted by this raw, grasping town or his appalling family, "a shame not his, and yet so unescapably his" (39). True, Merrick had never seemed happy; the public, Steavens remembers, had suspected wine or disappointed love. Steavens now knows that "the real tragedy of his master's life" lies in the town, "a desert of newness and ugliness and sordidness" (39), and even more in his home—the mother a grotesque, driven by violent emotions, her most striking feature large square teeth set far apart ("teeth that could tear" [36]),[32] and the father, sister, and abused servant, the mulatto Roxy, cowed and meek. Steavens senses the raw power emanating from the mother—even he feels himself being "drawn into the whirlpool" (36). What must Merrick have felt? The face in the coffin appears still resisting and struggling ("there was not that beautiful and chaste repose which we expect to find in the faces of the dead. . . . the chin was thrust forward defiantly . . . as though he were still guarding something precious, which might even yet be wrested from him" [36–37]).

Not only the life, but the art, Steavens now sees, bears the marks. He remembers that once Merrick had returned from a visit home bringing a "singularly feeling and suggestive bas-relief" (38). This piece, the only one described in the story, depicts a boy with a butterfly trying to catch the attention of a "thin, faded old woman" sitting sewing. Steavens had assumed the woman to be Merrick's mother, a guess that had brought a burning flush to the sculptor's face. Seeing the scarcely controlled brutality of the real Mrs. Merrick, Steavens understands the reason for the blush: the "tender and delicate modelling of the thin, tired face" in the sculpture was a sentimentalized vision, something other than truth. Perhaps the iconography of the bas-relief shows more: through the butterfly, an ancient symbol for the soul, Merrick may have been protesting the soul-destroying effect of early rejection and ignorance. That Cather meant to focus on this one piece of sculpture is indicated by a deletion she made when revising the story for republication of mention of another piece, entitled "Victory," as though to remove any indication that Merrick felt his success to be a final escape and triumph.[33]

Try though he may, the artist never truly leaves home. Dying, Merrick had said, "it rather seems as though we ought to go back to the place we came from in the end" (42).

The West of "The Sculptor's Garden" is not the world of the pioneers, but a later, less adventurous time of second- and third-generation money-grubbers, fixated on deal-making and gossip— "side-tracked, burnt-dog, land-poor sharks," Jim Laird calls them, in his final burst (again Cather resembles Twain). In contrast, The West of "A Wagner Matinee" is the harsh, backbreaking world of the first homesteaders.

Admirably condensed (the shortest in *The Troll Garden*), "A Wagner Matinee" is actually placed in Boston, where the narrator, Clark, a student, receives a visit from his aunt Georgiana, who took care of him in her frontier home when he was a motherless boy. She had once lived in Boston, a music teacher, and now she has made the trip from Nebraska to collect a small annuity. From his first sight of Georgiana's withered figure at the train station to the afternoon concert a few days later, when she sobs to him, as the concert hall empties, "I don't want to go!," Clark, in flashes of memory, recalls what her thirty years on the plains have been.

Bit by bit, a chronicle forms: the quarter section fifty miles from a railroad, measured by revolutions of a wagon wheel on which she and her new husband had tied a red handkerchief; the dugout, "one of those cave dwellings"; roving Indians; six children; her stiff fingers on a little parlor organ purchased after fifteen years and the "Gospel Hymns at Methodist service in the square frame school-house on Section Thirteen" (100); milking in the straw-thatched shed; sewing canvas mittens for the raw hands of the corn huskers; and over all "the inconceivable silence of the plains" (98). Left behind now, and ready to receive her again, is "the tall, unpainted house, with weather-curled boards; naked as a tower" (101).

The immense physical and psychic costs of civilizing the land are tangible. Aunt Georgiana wears "ill-fitting false teeth, and her skin was as yellow as a Mongolian's from constant exposure to a pitiless wind"

(96). Spiritually, too, she seems inert, or embalmed. At the concert, she first sits like a "granite Rameses in a museum" with the same aloofness as "old miners who drift into the Brown Hotel at Denver, . . . solitary as though they were still in a frozen camp on the Yukon" (98).

In a wonderful phrase—one belonging more to Clark's creator than to Clark—this cost is acknowledged: "the conquests of peace, dearer bought than those of war," have been purchased at great price (99). For Clark, it is a new and humbling realization ("I understand," he says, at the story's end, listening to his aunt sob). And it is newly felt, too, by Aunt Georgiana, as the music of the concert breaks down her stony exterior. The potency of art brings to both a moment of common suffering that, because it is mutual, is also comforting.

Not quite all the images of the West in this story are of deprivation and ugliness. A few suggestively link the two worlds of the story—the world of art and music and the world of the vast plains. Looking at the order and variety of the instruments of the orchestra, Clark remembers coming "fresh from ploughing forever and forever between green aisles of corn, where, as in a treadmill, one might walk from daybreak to dusk without perceiving shadow of change" (98); the violin bows "drove obliquely downward, like the pelting streaks of rain in a summer shower" (99); and when the orchestra leaves, the stage is "empty as a winter cornfield" (101). Here Cather hints, just hints, that there is a link between the austere beauty of the plains and the designs of musical form.

Dreadful though the years of toil have been, and continue to be, Georgiana's life and the story we read are not dispiriting. Watching his Aunt's resurgence of feeling as she listens to the afternoon concert, Clark meditates, "It never really died, then—the soul that can suffer so excruciatingly and so interminably; it withers to the outward eye only" (100). Aunt Georgiana has borne her fate stoically, even heroically. Clark had known this, and been superficially grateful for the love of music she had nurtured in him, but at the same time she had dwindled in his thoughts to a figure "at once pathetic and grotesque" (94). Now he sees her true worth.

Along with "Paul's Case" and "A Garden Lodge," but more explicitly, "A Wagner Matinee" confirms Cather's faith that art is necessary for the spirit, that without this gift, life dwindles into gray sameness. Among the wonderful touches in "A Wagner Matinee" are the contrasting musical sounds—so different, yet speaking to the same need: the soaring orchestral strains of the *Ring*, and behind these the reedy parlor organ, the Methodist hymns, an accordian belonging to a Norwegian farmhand, the idle singing of a tramp cowpuncher who, as a boy in Germany, had heard Wagner's "Prize Song."

The *Troll Garden* stories—the best of them—make clear that Cather was an accomplished short story writer before she moved to New York. They show, too, her abiding preoccupation with the topics troubling artists of her time: art versus illusion; the power of the imagination to synthesize, but also to distort; the relation of seeing to visualizing; the relation of art and nature.

Youth and the Bright Medusa

By 1918 Cather might have felt that her success as a writer was assured. She had published three novels, and her long story "The Bohemian Girl," which had come out in *McClure's*, was much admired. But she still felt insecure about her income, and she proposed to her editor at Houghton Mifflin that she publish a series of "light and breezy" stories about musicians and opera singers.[34] To the two already written, "The Diamond Mine" and "A Gold Slipper," she would add three or four others. The project came to nothing, partly because Cather shortly turned her attention to writing *My Ántonia*, but she revived it, in altered form, two years later when Alfred Knopf, her new publisher, proposed reissuing *The Troll Garden*. The book that came out in 1920, *Youth and the Bright Medusa*, is, then, something of a hybrid: it opens with four stories about singers, sprightly in tone, and concludes with four *Troll Garden* stories—"Paul's Case," "The Sculptor's Funeral," "A Wagner Matinee," and "'A Death in the Desert.'"

The first four, if not uniformly "light and breezy," have in common a knowing, sophisticated narrative voice, detached and a bit sardonic; it assumes familiarity with the world of the great *prime donne*, including the habits and manners of the society circling around these stars. Of the four, two, "The Diamond Mine" and "A Golden Slipper," are good, and one, "Coming, Aphrodite!" is great (this one, a lengthy story of young passion, will be discussed in the following chapter).

Cather had followed the international careers of famous singers since her student days in Lincoln. The years that she worked at *McClure's* and after were one of the great periods of the New York Metropolitan Opera Company, and Cather's friend Edith Lewis states that they went constantly, hearing Caruso, Mary Garden, Chaliapin, Tetrazzini. While writing feature articles for *McClure's*, first on the ballet and then on operatic voices, Cather found her way behind the scenes, where she met the Wagnerian soprano Olive Fremstad, who became her friend and served, in part, as the model for the singer-heroine of *The Song of the Lark*. Thus the pose of the cultivated and knowing observor that Cather assumes in these stories is authentic: she knew singers and the combination of temperament, control, and discipline their craft demands.

The Song of the Lark did not exhaust what Cather had to say about singers. What apparently fascinated Cather were the demands that a career in the public eye makes—the need to project the self, to charm, so different from the silence and solitude necessary to the painter or writer. She perceived the consuming attention to detail, the treatment of the self as artifact, that the art of performance entails.

The "diamond mine" in the story of that name is Cressida Garnet herself, who in the course of her long career supports a great number of persons "out of the mortal body of a woman"[35]—not only her inept and pretentious brother and sisters, but also a series of four husbands, a feckless son, and a Svengali-like voice coach, the Greek Jew Miletus Poppas. Carrie, the friend who tells the story, knew the Garnet family back in Columbus, Ohio, and encounters Cressida frequently enough to follow her fortunes. What Carrie extols is Cressida's "force of will" and "unabated vitality" (*YBM*, 72): "Her sterling character was the subject of her story" (88). Carrie skips over the first two husbands, one a boy who died young, the other a source of wealth, but not otherwise important; she devotes the longest section of the story to the third, the Czech composer Bouchalka, younger than Cressida, whom she rescues from obscurity and near starvation. Cressida seeks him out in his shabby rooming house, sees that his songs are given a hearing, introduces him to society, and marries him. Her very bounty is her undoing, for Bouchalka finds himself so comfortable and secure that he ceases to accompany his wife on her trying cross-country tours (her work at the Metropolitan dwindling) and finally is discovered in bed with the cook, more out of inertia, it would seem, than lust. He is regretfully dismissed. From him Cressida turns, somewhat later, to an ill-starred businessman whose investments never prosper. The story concludes as Carrie, knowing that Cressida has taken passage on the *Titanic*, goes to the White Star offices to search the list of survivors. There she sees four men waiting in Cressida's limousine: the brother, Buchanan; the son, Horace; the current husband; and Poppas.

A short epilogue tells us that the "mine" had been well-nigh exhausted. After payment of the fifty thousand–dollar bequest to Poppas (and Carrie, as executor, sees to it that Poppas receives his money, believing that to be Cressida's first intention) little is left, and that is fought over in endless legal battles by the remaining heirs. Cressida herself, it seemed, had awaited death fatalistically; no one reported seeing her on deck or in the lifeboats.

When this story came out, it was widely seen as a reference to the career of the singer Lillian Nordica, who had died in a shipwreck and whose will was contested with much publicity. The man figuring in the story as the last husband threatened a libel suit, but did not carry through.

There is a second source for this story, one that provides a clue to what emerges as the most significant of Cressida's ties. Though the story of Bouchalka looms largest in the telling, and largest in Cressida's feelings, a second relationship has supported her life in art. The resemblance of Poppas to Svengali, the hypnotic voice teacher in George du Maurier's notorious novel *Trilby*, is made explicit in the story, and indeed the most interesting question of the story is the nature of Poppas's power over Cressida. Carrie recalls that Cressida had not liked the novel, a sensation when it was published in 1894. "When 'Trilby' was published she fell into a fright and said such books ought to be prohibited by law; which gave me an intimation of what their relationship had actually become" (86). As Carrie knew, Poppas was essential from the beginning because "Cressida was not musically intelligent" (86); only with the help of Poppas's musicality and intelligence was she able to climb and cling to the heights of her profession. There is nothing sexual in the tie: when Bouchalka hints at such, he quickly acknowledges the implausability of such a charge (113). Poppas was simply indispensable: "He possessed a great many valuable things for which there is no market; intuition, discrimination, imagination, a whole twilight world of intentions and shadowy beginnings which were dark to Cressida" (86). To the relatives, the husbands, and even, at first, to Carrie, Poppas is an annoyance, an embarrassment, or worse—a "vulture," as Carrie terms him (75). Only after Cressida's death does Carrie appreciate his knowledge and devotion.

In *Trilby*, true to its Gothic style, the singer loses her voice with the death of Svengali. Cather cleverly reverses the situation: with Cressida's death, Poppas retires to the middle of Asia, as he always said he wanted to do, where it is always hot and dry, and his headaches from the wretched climate of New York and London will cease. From there—and this is the moment when Carrie sees into the long years of his devotion—he sends Carrie a verse, in German, that hints at the selflessness of his service. It is Carrie's sudden insight into Poppas's true role, she states, that "prompted this informal narration" (120). What is most proper and true, the poem hints ("Traulich und Treu"), is always found in the most profound and hidden depths ("der Tiefe").

Suddenly, the fairy-tale substructure of this story emerges. Poppas is the hidden gnome with the secret, the Rumpelstiltskin who can help the poor man's daughter spin the raw material of straw into the gold of art. He is Cressida's submerged self, in charge (bizarrely) of her very memories: "He was like a book in which she had written down more about herself than she could possibly remember—and it was information that she might need at any moment. He was the one person who knew her absolutely" (87).

Inescapably, we wonder why Cather chose a Jew to serve as the figure of the hidden, intuitive self, and further, why she stresses physical and racial stereotypical characteristics. As Carrie sees Poppas waiting in the limousine, she thinks he appears "old as Jewry" (118). It is ancientness, timeless endurance, that Cather is evoking: Poppas might be an Old Testament Jew, retiring to his "sainte Asie" (a holyland, perhaps [119]), a timeless realm. That he is a Greek Jew may indicate that Cather is linking the twin roots of Western myth, the classical and the Hebraic. Unfortunately, however, the description of Poppas has led some critics to the view that in this story Cather indulges in an underlying anti-Semitic bias, a view that obscures her many hints that Poppas represents the deep psychic levels that must be plumbed— mined, rather—before the diamond of art can be achieved.

Kitty Ayrshire in "A Gold Slipper" at first seems a lesser portrait, though elegantly executed. Where Cressida Garnet is magnificent and commanding, Kitty is flirtatious, her sexual charm a conscious part of her art. Her antagonist is Marshall McKann, a Pittsburgh businessman and Presbyterian (an upper-class version of Paul's father, as it were), a "person of substance, . . . solid and well-rooted" (123). They first meet on the stage of the Carnegie Music Hall, where Kitty is singing and where McKann, to his chagrin, finds himself seated with his wife and her dreaded artistic friend, Mrs. Post, when the concert managers add a series of folding chairs to accommodate the overflow audience. The velvet train of Kitty's gown (designed by a "conscienceless Pari-

sian" and "a little disconcerting, even to the well-disposed" [126–27])
brushes against his trouser leg as Kitty enters and leaves.

The sly humor of this story lies in the contrast of these two on the
Carnegie Hall stage—McKann, "hot and uncomfortable, in a chair
much too small for him, . . . among a lot of music students and excit-
able old maids," and Kitty, amused at the consternation her gown is
causing in this "hard-shelled" audience, assured that she will win back
their approval with her artistry (127). Much depends on that gown,
with its narrow train that "kept curling about her feet like a serpent's
tail, turning up its gold lining as if it were squirming over on its back,"
and on the "alarming" cut of the sleeves. When the "prehensile train
curled over his boot," McKann looks up to see Kitty's "bright, curious
eyes" rest on him for a second. During that second, McKann "beheld
himself a heavy, solid figure, unsuitably clad for the time and place,
with a florid, square face, well-visored with good living and sane opinions . . . , upon which years and feelings had made no mark—in which
cocktails might eventually blast out a few hollows" (129). But the self-
examination provoked by this brush with art is momentary. When they
meet a second time, as they do later on the overnight train to New
York, McKann's equanimity has been restored by a lunch at the
Schenley and a good cigar.

Their talk on the train comprises the second half of the story (it is
only a conversation—"A Gold Slipper" is not Mary McCarthy's "The
Man in the Brooks Brothers Shirt"). Kitty had seen him glower and
squirm at the concert, and she challenges McKann to say why he dis-
likes her and her kind, only to hear "you are, all of you, according to
my standards, light people. . . . You don't help to carry the burdens of
the world. You are self-indulgent and appetent" (140). At bottom, he
has a "natural distrust" of all art, artists, and their admirers as "fake"
(138–39). Kitty's defense is worth looking at closely: yes, she is self-
indulgent, but she gives pleasure to others and "something more" to
the "gifted" ones, those able to receive it: "my *wish*," which is "like
giving one's blood" (141). Warming in her argument, Kitty alludes to
"Count Tolstoy" ("I had a long talk with him once, about his book
'What is Art?'") and his belief that we are sad because "a divine ideal"
has been revealed to us, and given us "a new craving" so that "happiness lies in ceasing to be and to cause being, because the thing revealed to us is dearer than any existence our appetites can ever get for
us. I can understand that. It's something one often feels in art" (142).

But McKann is impervious. Tolstoy is a "crank," an extremist, and anyway, "McKann hated tall talk" (142–43). Then he delivers his final defense, his manner "judicial": "With a woman, everything comes back to one thing" (143). Though Kitty's poise is unshaken by the crass insult, her final pleasant good night takes the form of a subtle curse: "Anyhow, thank you for a pleasant evening. And, by the way, dream of me tonight, and not of either of those ladies who sat beside you" (146).

The next morning McKann, to his profound irritation, finds that she has flung him an added challenge: in the little hammock for clothes over his Pullman bed is a single gold slipper. The slipper eventually comes to rest in a lockbox in McKann's office vault, safe from prying eyes. McKann tells himself that he keeps it as "a reminder that absurd things could happen to people of the most clocklike deportment" (148)—an apt reference to people who live only in Bergson's chronological time. But physical instruments like clocks and vaults cannot contain the power emanating from this little slipper. Our last glimpse of McKann suggests a haunted man: ill and "sadly changed," he often puts the gold slipper on his desk and looks at it. He doesn't see in it any of the transcendent gifts of art that Kitty had tried to speak of (desire, or Tolstoy's divine ideal, or even simple pleasure); but "somehow it suggests life to his tired mind" (148). Where the more elevated lures fail, the memory of a beautiful woman wearing gold mesh stockings, gold slippers, and a gown with a prehensile train has persisted. Kitty has had her revenge.

"A Gold Slipper" is Cather's lightest story, but beneath its charm intriguing themes are introduced, notably the link between the potency of art and the power of sex. One senses throughout the pleasure Cather takes in Kitty—her elegance, her intelligence—and in planning McKann's richly deserved fall. (Kitty appears also in "Scandal," the fourth opera singer story, but here her personality is subdued, and the story is less successful.)

Cressida and Kitty are memorable women, strong and vibrant, bearing the deprivations their art entails with courage and style. Without them as standards, it would be harder to understand what Eden Bower chooses in her story, "Coming, Aphrodite!"

Four Love Stories

In "The Garden Lodge," Cather depicts her well-disciplined heroine, Caroline Noble, thinking disparagingly of sexual attraction and of that desire to which women owe "most of their mistakes and tragedies and astonishingly poor bargains" (*TG*, 52). In effect, Cather has been equated with Caroline's attempt to keep sexual passion at a cool distance. Cather's first biographer observes that " 'love,' in the conventional literary sense, scarcely figures in her novels."[36] Later commentators typically echo this generalization, finding that Cather neglects sexual passion, either out of overnicety (her "bluff, middy blouse suspicions of both sexuality and vulgarity," as one writer puts it) [37] or, a reason common in later criticism, out of repressed sexual fears in her personal life ("normal sex stands barred from her fictional world").[38] Those biographers who assume a lesbian orientation look for, and find, evidence for same-sex attractions behind her fictional relationships.[39] However all this may be, her writings of all kinds, especially the letters that have survived, make clear that Cather's nature was deep feeling, indeed ardent. She had warm and enduring attachments to family, friends (old and new, male and female), even business relations—she flung her arms around S. S. McClure when they met after many years, and she had a loyal, thoughtful friend in the publisher Alfred Knopf. There was nothing of the cool recluse in the way she entered human relationships. This capacity for passionate attachment gives intensity to the few stories she wrote in which a love interest is central.

"Coming, Aphrodite!"

"Coming, Aphrodite!" clearly shows both Cather's awareness of the play of erotic energies and her skill in conveying these tensions. The story itself, one of Cather's best, is solely concerned with the advent of passionate love; in addition, its printing history provides evidence that Cather was consciously pushing the limits of sexual explicitness for that time. To make the story acceptable for magazine publication in 1920, Cather altered the text in a number of ways, making the affair more a matter of implication and toning down the sensual overtones in her descriptions.[40]

Opera buffs of the time would have seen in the title an allusion that we now miss, as Mary Garden, the first true American diva, had recently appeared in the role of Aphrodite in Erlanger's opera of that name. Quite apart from that information, however, readers would see in the title "Coming, Aphrodite!" (changed for magazine publication to "Coming, Eden Bower!") the promise that a story of erotic love would follow.

The setting is a rooming house on New York's Washington Square just after the turn of the century, "almost the very last summer of the old horse stages on Fifth Avenue" (*YBM*, 2). The leisureliness and ease of the great city in summer creates the right background for the brief love affair between the reclusive painter Don Hedger and Eden Bower (born Edna Bowers of Huntington, Illinois), who moves into the room next to Hedger's. Cather had lived on Washington Square the first year she worked in New York, and the handsome square (as it then was) with its arch and fountain, the nearby Brevoort Hotel, oyster houses, and basement restaurants all appear in the story.

Hedger and his bulldog, Caesar III, have lived here in a third-floor studio for four years, content with the dim north light that painters prefer. Even among self-sufficient artists, Hedger is a loner. Brought up in a school for homeless boys, he has educated himself through travel and by following his bent wherever it might lead. He is meticulous only about his painting and his dog, who "was invariably fresh and shining" (4). Although Hedger hears Eden's trunk and piano being moved in, he does not meet her until one day, emerging from bathing Caesar in the floor's one bathroom, he finds "a tall figure in a flowing blue silk dressing gown" who says, "I wish you wouldn't wash your dog in the tub. I never heard of such a thing! I've found his hair in the tub, and I've smelled a doggy smell, and now I've caught you at it" (14). Hedger is badly confused, and faced with "her white arms and neck and her fragrant person" something flashes through his mind "about a man who was turned into a dog or was pursued by dogs, because he unwittingly intruded upon the bath of beauty" (15).

Hedger's next brush with Eden—a peculiarly one-way encounter—occurs as he is cleaning out the clothes closet separating their two rooms. Without thinking, Hedger stoops to squint through a knothole to the other side, where, in a pool of sunlight, wholly unclad, Eden is going through an exercise routine. Accustomed though he is to the sight of the nude female body, Hedger feels that a piece of charcoal would explode in a hand trying to capture "the energy of each gesture . . . discharged into the whirling disc of light" (18). Day after day Hedger crouches amid the old shoes in his closet, oblivious to manners or morals: "Hedger scarcely regarded his action as conduct at all; it was something that had happened to him. . . . It was a heathenish feeling; without friendliness, almost without tenderness" (31). He has no desire to meet the Miss Bower "who wore shirt-waists and got letters from Chicago," who practices Puccini and goes out with young men wearing white flannel suits and carrying canes. His business is with "a room full of sun, a little enchanted rug of sleeping colours, and a woman who emerged naked through a door, and disappeared naked. He thought of that body as never having been clad . . . for him she had no geographical associations; unless with Crete, or Alexandria, or Veronese's Venice. She was the immortal conception, the perennial theme" (22). The link to Venus is underscored by Eden's delight in watching a flock of pigeons (not quite Venus's doves) soar and wheel over the square about five every afternoon. Hedger and Eden speak, finally, about these pigeons, and their acquaintance grows.

Cather's particular achievement in this story lies in how she conveys the growing intimacy of Hedger and Eden. It is a mutual courtship, not a series of advances by the male: a primitive mating ritual, full of preening, yet challenging and wary, its pace like the crescendo of two flamenco dancers.

Eden performs first. On a Sunday she agrees to go with Hedger to Coney Island, where one of his models, Molly Welch, is scheduled to make a balloon ascent, a stunt that adds to her earnings. Besides, Hedger says, it is nice to see "tailors and bar-tenders and prize-fighters with their best girls, and all sorts of folks taking a holiday" (33). Not Eden's people at all. She can't say why she likes this funny painter, with his black eyebrows. But that afternoon they watch the balloon together as the bathers cheer, the band plays, and the girl in green tights steps out of the basket and sways on a trapeze. "Not many girls would look well in that position," says Hedger, and then blushes a "slow, dark, painful crimson" (36). Eden stays in the tent with Molly as she gets ready for the second ascent, but when the balloon finally bumps off, the crowd sees that it is a new girl—"You're a peach, girlie," they call (37). As Hedger, dripping with cold sweat, watches, Eden goes through the whole act: she takes off the black evening skirt, descends on the trapeze in black tights and silver slippers, and floats down on the beach, a "slowly falling silver star"—a Venus emerging from the foam (39).

Now it is Hedger's turn. But he doesn't answer with a comparable show of bravado; instead, as Eden sips champagne in the restaurant where they go for dinner, he tells her a grim story, an Aztec rain legend called "The Forty Lovers of the Queen," which he once heard from a Mexican priest in the Southwest.

In a well-known observation about the structure of her novel *The Professor's House*, Cather said that by inserting a novella into its midst she was using a technique suggested by Dutch genre painters who show a window to the outer world in their interiors—"the masts of ships or a stretch of grey sea" (*OW*, 31). It is such a device that Cather also uses in "Coming, Aphrodite!": Hedger's legend is a chilling glimpse of a cold, dangerous current, unlike the warm surf at Coney Island or Venus's silvery foam. This aspect of Venus—"the perennial theme"—is dark, hinting at compulsive desire, pain, and danger.

One day a beautiful Indian princess, who has been dedicated to the rain gods, sees among a group of warrior prisoners a young chief, taller than all the rest, with arms and breast covered with the figures of wild animals "bitten into the skin and coloured" (43). The princess begs the young chief's life, and asks him to "prick upon her skin the signs of Rain and Lightning and Thunder, and stain the wounds with herb juices" (43). For many days the princess submitted to the bone needle, and the women of the tribe wondered at her courage. Before the tattoo artist she had no shame, and one day the guardians called in alarm that he had fallen upon her "to violate her honour" (43). For this crime he is gelded, his tongue is torn out, and he is given to the princess, now married and a queen, as her slave. She orders the slave to bring to her chosen lovers, and then to lead them away through a cavern where one stone has been loosened so that they fall through into a cold underground river. The story ends with the execution by fire of both the queen and the slave when, out of jealousy of a lover growing in favor, the slave tells the king of the queen's infidelities—"and afterward there was a scarcity of rain" (46).

Hedger was not trying to please her, Eden thinks. "He was testing her, trying her out" (46). Back in her room, she cannot sleep: "Crowds and balloons were all very well, she reflected, but woman's chief adventure is man" (47). She climbs the steep ladder to the tenement roof for fresh air, and as she steps through the trap door, the bulldog's sharp little teeth catch her ankle. Her courage roused, so it seems, by the teeth, Eden stays on the roof with Hedger and they become lovers. Some days later, at Eden's suggestion, they break open the doors between their rooms. Eden takes up a bronze Buddha and strikes the painted bolt with the idol's "squatting posteriors" (50). They seem to know that their happiness will not last. "I won't always be the only one, Eden Bower," Hedger says; "What does that matter? You are the first," she answers.

The end comes abruptly. Eden, whose taste in painting runs to "Christ Before Pilate and a redhaired Magdalen" (27), urges Hedger to let her introduce him to a "successful" painter. She doesn't understand his fury, or his contention that he already has the luxury he wants, the luxury of being able "to please nobody but myself" (52). Hedger leaves, but after five days he rushes back, only to find Eden gone: a sudden chance to study abroad. For Hedger, "it was as if tigers were tearing him" (57), or like the biting hounds he had dimly sensed on first seeing Eden.

From an epilogue, set eighteen years later, we learn that both Eden and Hedger are successful artists, though in their different ways. Hedger is a painter's painter, "the first man among the moderns," the gallery dealer tells Eden, when she inquires. As Eden's limousine drives away, the street lamps flash on a hard and settled face, "like a plaster cast" (63). But tomorrow, on the stage, it will be the "golden face of Aphrodite." The Medusa of art has transmuted the passion and energy of life into a settled form. Eden is now an artifact, a conduit for beauty and love.[41]

Though the story maintains a consistently light, even mildly satiric, narrative tone, the images it leaves in the mind are intense, lurid, like those in an expressionist painting: a carnival balloon, an artist-voyeur, death in a cold river. The boldest is the sharp tattooer's needle (felt again as the dog's teeth seize Eden, or when the tigers tear at Hedger), where the union of art and sex is made explicit in the pictures "bitten in the skin." These images, and all of the other narrative devices Cather uses—the game-playing tone, motifs from legend and myth, animal imagery (the identification of Hedger and his dog), and the context of sharply contrasting urban scenes—strongly identify her as an artist working in the idiom of her time. Included in this idiom is erotic knowing, an acknowledgment of love's golden moments, its ambiguities (she had read her friend D. H. Lawrence), and its desolations.

Part 1

"Eric Hermannson's Soul" and "The Bohemian Girl"

Cather often made fun of the conventional love story, but in "Eric Hermannson's Soul" and "The Bohemian Girl" she comes close to the popular journalistic fiction of the time. She sold both to magazines, but never included them in later collections. In truth, they suffer from overwriting ("ah! across what leagues of land and sea, by what improbable chances, do the unrelenting gods bring us our fate!" [*CSF*, 362]), their chief interest being the tug between East and West, art and life, or love, as these tensions were playing out in Cather's imagination.

The better of the two, "Eric Hermannson's Soul," is early (1900)—Cather's first really accomplished piece of fiction. The setting is the Divide, the bleak high land near Red Cloud that Cather knew so well and had used for her earliest student attempts, sketches about the effects of terrible solitude on the early settlers. The love affair is between Eric Hermannson, a blond young giant, who emigrated from the north of Norway with his mother when he was eighteen, and Margaret Elliot, from New York, "beautiful, talented, critical, unsatisfied, tired of the world at twenty-four" (363). She is engaged to be married, and has come West with her brother Wyllis for a last taste of freedom: "It comes to all women of her type—that desire to taste the unknown which allures and terrifies, to run one's whole length out to the wind—just once" (363).

A love story about a girl from the East and a brawny Westerner was by 1900 a cliché (though Owen Wister's *The Virginian* had yet to be written). What lifts Eric Hermannson's story above the banal is that Cather supplies a countering plot, Eric's conversion by a frontier preacher, that adds a dimension to his avowals of which Margaret, in her sophistication, is scarcely aware. The story begins, "It was a great night at the Lone Star schoolhouse—a night when the Spirit was present with power and when God was very near to man. So it seemed to Asa Skinner, servant of God and Free Gospeller" (359). The descriptions of Asa, shouting of mercy and vengeance, and the men and women "trembling and quailing" before the power of some mysterious psychic force are free of rhetorical excess. The excess is all Asa's as he exhorts Eric, "the wildest lad on all the Divide," to come to the mourners' bench: "*Lazarus, come forth!* Eric Hermannson, you are lost, going down at sea. In the name of God, and Jesus Christ his Son, I throw you the life line. Take hold! Almighty God, my soul for his!" And so

Eric, with a groan "like the groan of a great tree when it falls in the forest," comes forward and breaks the neck of his violin (the very incarnation of evil desires for the Free Gospellers)—"and to Asa Skinner the sound was like the shackles of sin broken audibly asunder" (362).

Eric keeps his sworn faith for two years, until he goes for a week to help Jerry Lockhart thresh and hears Margaret pumping on Mrs. Lockhart's old parlor organ. She plays for him the intermezzo from *Cavalleria Rusticana* (no doubt this knowing girl takes pleasure in the aptness of playing this music to a rustic cowboy), and then, in a scene that points ahead to "A Wagner Matinee," she is unexpectedly moved by the "tears in his voice" as he tells her that he had never known there was music like that in the world. "Think of it," Margaret says later to her brother, "to care for music as he does and never to hear it, never to know that it exists on earth!" (366). But it cannot occur to her that for a segment of Eric's world music is a danger to the soul.

Two scenes convey the growing passion between Eric and Margaret without exceeding the limits permissible in magazine fiction of the time. In the first, rearing, scarcely tamed horses, imagery as classical as Hedger's biting hounds, but here merging realistically into the Western setting, portray their roused feelings. Eric accompanies Margaret on a ride to the next town for mail, and on the way home, a herd of wild mustangs, their drivers negligent, tempt Margaret's and Eric's horses to run. In a scene of great intensity, Eric subdues the biting, kicking animals, then openly declares his love in language that sounds extravagant, though he speaks simple truth: "You are the only beautiful thing that has come close to me. . . . I love you more than Christ who died for me, more than I am afraid of hell, or hope for heaven" (372).

Back in her bedroom in the ranch house, Margaret reads a long, bored letter from her fiancé, in which he complains that the actress playing Rosalind in an amateur production of *As You Like It* "insists on reading into the part all sorts of deeper meanings . . . wholly out of harmony with the pastoral setting" (373). The irony, though perhaps too obvious, is powerful in expressing the theme of this story, the impossible distance between West (energy, raw feeling) and East (beauty, art, understanding).

At the close of the story, Margaret arranges—to please herself—a farewell dance party at the ranch house, and here Eric picks up the violin again, playing folk songs from the North, and dances ("no longer the big, silent Norwegian who had sat at Margaret's feet. . . . Tonight he was Siegfried indeed" [375]). In a memorable scene, the last between Eric and Margaret, he takes her from the dance and together they climb the windmill, as other couples have done, to be alone and to feel the closeness of the Western sky. Stung by the appeal in his eyes, Margaret kisses Eric, and knows "that such love comes to one only in dreams or in impossible places like this, unattainable always" (378). It is the romantic's yearning cry, and it has a peculiar appropriateness here "on a windmill tower at the world's end" (377).

Cather ends the story with another outpouring of anguished feeling, though from another world, as Asa Skinner, "pale and worn with looking after his wayward flock," confronts the unrepentant Eric: "And it is for things like this that you set your soul back a thousand years from God. O foolish and perverse generation!" (379).

"The Bohemian Girl," written twelve years later, was sold for a good price, helping Cather decide that she could live by her writing. More slackly written than "Eric Hermanson's Soul," and almost twice as long, it is set in the West of a later time: the Norwegian immigrants who had crowded into Asa Skinner's meetings "driven by toil and saddened by exile" (360) have been transformed into the prosperous Ericson family—eight sons with farms of their own, and high-handed Old Lady Ericson, who takes pleasure in driving her new automobile herself, living on the old place with her last son, the boy Eric.

The gulf between West and East is no longer unbridgeable, and indeed the terms have taken on different meanings, connoting character types: the East gaiety-loving, musical, and unconventional, the West property-loving, slow, and conventional.

The story opens with the return of Nils, the Ericson prodigal, who had run away twelve years before—run very far East, to Sweden and Norway, where he works for a Bergen ship line. He has begun to remember Clara Vavrika, his "Bohemian girl," and he tries to win her back, never mind that she is now his sister-in-law, having married his brother Olaf in response to community pressure when Nils stopped writing her. Nils tells her about life in easygoing Stockholm: "Sit out in the streets in front of cafés and talk all night in summer. . . . Jolliest people in the world, the Swedes, once you get them going . . . . Always drinking things—champagne and stout mixed, half-and-half" (*CSF*, 33).

In contrast are the stolid Ericsons, especially Olaf, who will soon sit in the legislature, "weighing a thousand tons" (35). Nils sets about to pry Clara loose, visiting her at home and at her father's, Joe Vavrika's pleasant saloon. He plays his flute while Clara plays the piano, and dances with her at Olaf's barn raising. Finally, on a moonlit night, he intercepts her horseback ride and persuades her to leave with him that night. Her mettlesome horse (she is most often seen riding restlessly across the country) becomes a symbol of her passion (as for Margaret Elliot), and as Clara struggles to decide whether to run away with Nils or to stay, the land she loves pulls one way ("The great silent country seemed to lay a spell upon her") and the waiting horses another ("Beside her she heard the tramping of horses in the soft earth" [38]). The scene ends with "a thud of hoofs along the moonlit road, two dark shadows going over the hill; and then the great, still land stretched untroubled under the azure night" (38).

Cather is very easy on her careless lovers. Nils, handsome and engaging, seems untroubled by having neglected to write Clara, and completely untroubled about running off with his brother's wife. Clara is spoiled and willful, her old aunt Joanna having all the care of the housework. They escape to live happily, carrying no burden of guilt or regret. Their fathers are on their side: Joe Vavrika receives letters from Clara about their travels in Bohemia, and Nils's father, before he died, had secretly sent Nils money. Only Mrs. Ericson is harsh and unforgiving: she forbids young Eric to speak to Vavrika, and the closing incident of the story is in a minor key: Nils has sent Eric money to join him in Bergen, and Eric starts on the journey, but stumbles off the train at the last minute, unable to bear the thought of his mother alone on the farm. Not everyone who wishes can escape.

The theme of escape from the West (this time a small town) appears in another story written shortly before "The Bohemian Girl"—"The Joy of Nelly Deane." Moments in the story are haunting: a kind of *Erlkönig* fatality hangs over bright, pretty Nelly (like Clara, a fount of energy and lightness). Her avenue of escape is her secret engagement to a traveling salesman from Chicago. A sexually charged life force in her responds imaginatively to "the great city pulsing across the miles of snow, . . . throbbing like great engines" (*CSF*, 61). Jilted by her salesman, Nelly marries Scott Spinny, the hardware merchant, whose strong, cold hands are hard "like the castings he sold" (58). He has dogged Nelly since she was a girl, like a nemesis, or like death, prefigured further in Nelly's induction into the Baptist church—total immersion into the waters of a cement pit at the front of the church. As she rises from the dark water, three Baptist ladies, the ominously named Mrs. Dow, Mrs. Freeze, and Mrs. Spinny, receive her. It comes as no surprise that Nelly dies a few years later of neglect in childbirth. The ironic title of this story seems to point to entrapment in the West as a death, even though Nelly's vitality and joy in life continue in her little girl.

It is worth noting that, although Cather later wrote sympathetically of religion and religious feeling, for example in the novels *My Mortal Enemy* or *Death Comes for the Archbishop*, she pictures organized religion in her early work as stifling: Presbyterian Calvinism in "Paul's Case" and "A Gold Slipper," evangelical revivals in "Eric Hermannson's Soul," and the Baptist church in "The Joy of Nelly Deane." It appears that Cather gradually included religious aspiration and experience as akin to, or the same as, aesthetic experience, which she always spiritualized (Eric's violin was "his only bridge into the kingdom of the soul" [361]). In this equating of art and religion as avenues for spiritual energy she would have been following Henri Bergson, who speaks of the similarity of great artists and saints, both able to break into the flow of duration where others are oblivious.[42]

In "The Bohemian Girl" Cather makes a distinction, made before but less explicitly, that is important for her later work: the West of the land—the yellow fields, the poplar groves, the white rivers of dust—is set apart from the dull people, the generations who succeeded the pioneers, now weighing it down. Only a few see the land freely without wanting to master and possess it. Clara is one. The land itself, not her family attachments, calls to her, urging her to stay. In the novels Cather was shortly to write—*O Pioneers!*, *The Song of the Lark*, and *My Ántonia*—this love of the land dominates, but its people, even small-town people, would be included.

"Eric Hermannson's Soul" and "The Bohemian Girl" interest us for the primacy they give to erotic attraction, and for the link they suggest between sexual energy and artistic sensibility, but they also record how the West was filtering through Cather's imagination.

"Uncle Valentine"

"Uncle Valentine" remains the most puzzling of Cather's major stories, although critics who comment on the short fiction treat it respectfully and admire its portraits, its even, autumnal tone, and its word pictures.[43] Certainly it shows careful, deliberate workmanship. By 1925, when "Uncle Valentine" was written, Cather was a fully established author and was not writing magazine stories to sell. Indeed, she wrote few stories after 1920.

"Uncle Valentine" pretends to be a memoir, written in a somewhat meandering style, about a magnetic personality, the musician Valentine Ramsey. It is clear that Cather is modeling him on the composer Ethelbert Nevin, who had been an important figure for her during her early years in Pittsburgh (he was the first famous artist she knew well). She wrote about Nevin in her pieces for the Nebraska journals and in letters to friends, and her rapt admiration shines through both. The similarities between her view of Nevin and of her fictional Valentine are clear. For example, this characterization of Nevin could well apply to Valentine: "He had been unable to place any sort of non-conducting medium between the world and himself, no sort of protection to break the jar of things."[44]

Imitating the memoir frame, Cather takes as her narrator a girl, Marjorie, who at sixteen had been fascinated by her "uncle" Valentine. In the first scene of the story, Marjorie, now a mature woman, visits the Paris studio of Louise Ireland, once an intimate of Valentine, who is giving a voice lesson. A song she is teaching brings back the "golden year" when Valentine was a neighbor.

The story's leisurely form—thirteen short numbered parts—resembles a mind recalling loosely associated scenes from a lost past: musical evenings, walks, teas, a Christmas Eve. The subtitle, "Adagio non troppo," suggests also a musical form, and Cather may have had in mind a song cycle (Nevin composed songs somewhat in the manner of Schubert), or a tone poem (Wagner, Debussy, and Saint-Saëns are mentioned in the story). Cather maintains a tone of delicate melancholy throughout, viewing the events, such as they are, through a scrim of idyll and sentiment; a problem of the story, in fact, is whether the sentiment may be too indulgent.

A lost place as well as a lost time is evoked. Cather as a young woman had been a guest of Nevin and his wife at their estate, Vineacre, in the hills outside Pittsburgh, and she recreates this ambience as Greenacre, a rural area enclosing the Ramsay estate, Bonnie Brae, and its close neighbor, Fox Hill, the home of the Waterfords, where Marjorie lives with her aunt Charlotte. Its gardens, orchards, and hay fields form a refuge—a temporary one—from the encroaching dark, satanic mills of industrial Pittsburgh. There is a feel of old, perhaps Southern, aristocracy about Greenacre.

As always, it is a mistake to read Cather too literally. True, she is paying homage to an admired figure, but she goes to considerable trouble to rework her material and to frame her central figure. Her focus, I think, is the love that Valentine (surely a significant name, even though prefixed by a thoroughly unromantic term of relationship) inspires in women. It may be relevant that Adriance Hilgarde, the composer in "'A Death in the Desert,'" thought to be Cather's first attempt to portray Nevin, is also supremely attractive to women.

Marjorie first tries to portray Aunt Charlotte, though she says, significantly, that "it was not until years afterward, not until after her death, indeed, that I began really to know her" (*UVOS*, 8)—that is, to realize that the affection between Charlotte and Valentine was love, or the memory of an earlier, hopeless love.[45] At the time of the story Charlotte is in her midthirties (ten years older than Valentine), married to Harry Waterford (not unhappily), the mother of four girls, and the guardian of Marjorie and her sister. Marjorie remembers her special qualities: she only cautiously made any change in her beloved house, where she was born, as though she was afraid of losing something; she had "wonderful taste" (Marjorie adds, surely speaking in Cather's voice, "Our old friends considered taste as something quite apart from intelligence, instead of the flower of it" [8]); her love of music was a "way of living" ("what other people learned from books she learned from music" [9]).

Charlotte had known Valentine since he was a child, and watched over him after his mother died. She had not approved of his early marriage to Janet Oglethorpe, of the enormously rich Pittsburgh Oglethorpes. The marriage had failed. Leaving his wife in Italy, Valentine ran off with the beautiful and notorious Louise Ireland. Janet is remarried, living again in Pittsburgh. Now Valentine has returned from abroad in mild disgrace to live again next door in that strange household of men—his aging father, Jonathan; his Uncle Roland, who had once been a musical prodigy; and his older brother, Morton, who still makes a pretense of going to work in the city, though persistent drinking means that his accountants need to repair his figures at the end of each day. They are tyrannized by their Swedish housekeeper, Molla Carlsen. Roland's career came to nothing, and a sense of doom can be felt whenever he is present, his death-in-life existence suggesting what could happen to Valentine were his talents to fail.

But during the "golden year" Valentine's talents flourish, following the arid years of his marriage. Under the influence of his beloved gardens, hills, and woods—and under the influence of Charlotte—he writes the thirty songs for which he is best remembered. Marjorie's memory, moving through the year from November to the next autumn, picks up scene after scene of Charlotte and Valentine, despite the fact that, as Marjorie recalls, "she almost never saw him alone" (17). They do have one excursion together, a trip into the city at Christmas time (Cather had had just such a shopping expedition with Nevin [Woodress, 359]), and when they return "their faces shone like the righteous in his Heavenly Father's house" (16). It is after that day that Valentine begins to compose, his first song the "Ballad of the Young Knight," beginning "From the Ancient Kingdoms, / Through the woods of dreaming, . . ." Valentine wrote both music and words for his compositions, "like the old troubadours" (19).

Gradually, the pattern of the love between Charlotte and Valentine emerges: it is the legendary one—the fated love of the young knight for the queen. It is only for Charlotte that he can write: as a schoolboy, he says, he neglected lessons, probably "writing serenades for you, Charlotte" (12). When he was a boy Valentine had been "her squire" (6), and later when Harry Waterford came courting "the spoiled neighbor boy was always hanging about" (6). Music is their love, and Wagner their passion: "Charlotte, do you remember how we used to play the Ring to each other hours on end, long ago, when Damrosch first brought German opera over?"(25).

One day, on a walk in the hills, as the mist drifts over the water and Charlotte and Valentine breathe together "The Rhinegold," something in the two voices awes even the little girls. Later Valentine plays the Rhine music "as if he would never stop" (25). (During 1925 Cather also wrote a preface for the republication of a book on Wagner's operas, so that his romantic themes would have been much on her mind; see *OW* 60–66). The significance of Wagner's music is underscored by Valentine's recollection of an incident in his marriage—almost a comic anecdote: he had thought to escape to Bayreuth, but Janet had pursued him and arrived in the middle of the Ring. "My God, the agony of having to sit through music with that woman!" (13).

An evening in full summer, when there was "a languorous spirit of beauty abroad—warm, sensuous, oppressive, like the pressure of a warm, clinging body" (29), gives fullest expression to their frustration. Marjorie looks for Charlotte, who speaks impatiently, "I can't be with anyone tonight" (29), and Valentine sends her abruptly away. The next day he goes into the city. He has been hearing from Louise Ireland (five purple letters received at once), but when he returns he announces to Charlotte that he is not leaving ("I do seem to be tied to you" [31]). She "looked radiantly happy" (30).

It is probable that Charlotte has been a faithful wife ("her life was hedged about by very subtle and sure conventionalities" [27]). Still, Harry once makes an odd comment to her about the roses he cultivates on a retaining wall, "I like their being without an odor; it gives them a kind of frankness and innocence." Charlotte flushes at the peculiar use of the word: "Innocence? . . . I shouldn't call it just that" (28).

The golden, timeless year ends abruptly. In the autumn Valentine and the Waterfords learn that the large neighboring estate, long empty, has been sold, and on a walk they meet the purchasers—Janet and her husband. Valentine feels hunted and trapped, and in truth Janet appears something of an ogress, with a red, shiny face and "teeth too far apart, something crude and inelegant about them" (35). (We recall the same feature in the awful Mrs. Merrick.) Her reason for moving nearby, however, seems laudable—she wishes their son to know the Ramsay relatives. Valentine behaves rudely and excessively, as is his usual style. Like the real Nevin, he had in his character "no sort of protection to break the jar of things." In November he leaves, and two years later he is accidentally killed by a motor truck near Louise Ireland's apartment.

The twilit world of "Uncle Valentine" resembles the robust world of "Coming, Aphrodite!" hardly at all. They are alike only in reiterating Cather's belief that the life given to art can have little to do with life's ordinary passages—"marriage, money, friends, the general social order," as Louise Ireland lists them (3). The distinction of the *Troll Garden* stories persist, as Cather moves from the social concerns of the earlier fiction to more abstract, philosophical patterns. "Aesthetics come back to predestination, if theology doesn't," Valentine tells Charlotte, emphasizing the other-worldly mystery—inexplicable, anarchic—that attaches not only to artistic creation, but to the phenomenon of beauty itself, and those sensitive to beauty. Wagner's myth that the Rhine gold can be possessed only by one who renounces love seems to underlie Valentine's strange character: he inspires love—Charlotte, Louise, even Janet, and possibly the young Marjorie—but accepts none fully. The distortions imposed by a life given to art is a theme Cather will turn to again in almost her last story, "The Old Beauty."

The charge that Cather ignores the erotic is a serious one, but not, I think, a justified one, as these four stories demonstrate.

"for which the first was made": *Obscure Destinies*

The three stories comprising *Obscure Destinies*—"Neighbour Rosicky," "Old Mrs. Harris," and "Two Friends"—represent the peak of Cather's accomplishment in this form. Although each story stands by itself, all have the same Nebraska locale, the places and persons of her girlhood that Cather remembered with such luminous exactitude. They blend seamlessly with the earlier works based on Red Cloud memories—*The Song of the Lark, My Ántonia,* "The Enchanted Bluff"—though the town of the story may be placed in Colorado or Kansas. The fact that Cather's youthful self is a character in two of the stories adds to our sense that she is looking back intently at pictures long harbored in her imagination.

Cather's father died in 1928, and during the following four years, as Cather worked on these stories and on her novel *Shadows on the Rock,* her mother lay ill and dying. A sense of life's transiency, but also of its completeness, underlies all three short stories: in two, a death follows a long life, and in the third a narrative coda tells us how the two friends died.

Cather's topic is time itself, in the double aspect that Bergson explored—in human terms, its ravages and its transformations. In each of the stories (though only faintly in "Rosicky") a moment occurs when the narrative voice moves suddenly to a new and distant perspective, holding the time of the story in its grasp. Paul Ricoeur, in his treatise on temporality in narrative, speaks of "aporias" in the experience of time, disorienting disjunctions in perspective.[46] A famous—the most famous—literary example is the removal of Troilus to the eighth sphere at the end of Chaucer's poem, so that we see Troilus look back on his life, with all its intensities, and watch it dim and fade. Closer to our time, Thornton Wilder's *Our Town,* a work Cather liked, dramatizes the disjunction. Chaucer relies on clear medieval cosmology, and Wilder has his characters speak from beyond the grave. Cather works more ambiguously. In her stories, the long perspective is still within time, tied to the persons and things of the objective world, with only a hint of transcendence.

"Neighbour Rosicky"

"Neighbour Rosicky" is a portrait of the last year of Rosicky's life, more precisely of Rosicky remembering his life—remembering it not nostalgically but actively and purposefully, mining it to form the future. It is a picture of the interpenetration of the past and the present, of the world being made, a Bergsonian concept fictionalized.

In the first scene, Rosicky comes to town to make a professional call on his friend Doctor Ed, who tells him that he should pamper his bad heart and leave the heavy work of the farm to his sons. Rosicky can afford this; he has willing sons and a loving wife. But he worries about Rudolf, his oldest son, who has recently married and is trying to make a go of farming on his own. Rudolf's wife, Polly, is a town girl, not used to the farm or Bohemian ways, and Rosicky fears that another drought will drive them from the land. In his life, full of hardship, Rosicky has found that poverty itself is bearable; what is truly "terrifying and horrible" is "the look in the eyes of a dishonest and crafty man, or a scheming and rapacious woman," sights he associates with city living.[47] Once in his life Rosicky had to take money from the hand of a hungry child, because it was owed his employer. He wants his sons to be spared this dreadfulness.

Rosicky sets about making Polly's life more pleasant. He washes her dishes and loans Rudolf the car for a Saturday night at the picture show. Most important, he tells them a story.

Rosicky has lived in three countries: first in Bohemia, on land his grandparents worked; then in England, where as a young man he lived in London; and finally in America, where he stayed in New York for fifteen years, working as a tailor, until his feeling for the land and growing things drove him to risk moving to the opening fields of Nebraska as a farm hand. At Christmas Rosicky tells Rudolf and Polly the story of his Christmas in London, a time full of such wretchedness that he has left it buried, "a sore spot in his mind that wouldn't bear touching" (*OD*, 27). But "he wanted Polly to hear this one" (51). He describes his life as a tailor's apprentice, living in a curtained-off corner of his employer's flat, and tells how, driven by cold and hunger, he woke at night and ate the family's Christmas dinner goose before he could stop himself. Walking the streets in despair, he is miraculously rescued by four strangers, to whom he appeals when he hears them speaking Czech. These travelers from the east give him money to replace the Christmas dinner, and later aid him to leave for America. It is a story of deprivation and humiliation—also of deliverance—and it touches Polly. That the memory Rosicky uses is a Christmas story told on Christmas day suggests an extension of meaning. Not personal memory alone, but the commemorative recollection—the common human pattern of remembrance and renewal—is being tapped. Another anecdote embedded in the story suggests this same pattern. Rosicky remembers that it was on the Fourth of July, sitting in Park Place, when he realized that big cities "built you in from the earth itself, cemented you away from any contact with the ground" (31). That was when he decided to risk moving West. Later, we learn of another Fourth of July. Rosicky's wife, Mary, recalls a time when the boys were little, and the terrible prairie heat had just killed that year's crops, and how Rosicky insisted anyhow on a celebration. While the Methodists were gathering in the church to pray for rain, Rosicky stayed at home, frolicked in the horse tank with his boys, and picnicked on chicken under the young mulberry trees. Personal memories blend with larger sacred and communal rituals to renew and give hope. In William James's terms, Rosicky is of heroic mold, heroes being those persons who not only face fate but embrace it, who celebrate even as the crops wither.

Rosicky dies from a heart attack brought on by raking Russian thistles from Rudolf's alfalfa, a field Rosicky loves because "when he was a little boy, he had played in fields of that strong blue-green colour" (62). His attachment to the beauty of the field, his desire to preserve it, overrides any consideration for his own life. Stricken in the field, Rosicky leans on Polly. As she helps him to bed and cares for him, she senses his "special gift for loving people, something that was like an ear for music" (66). It was something like an "awakening" to her (69). Rosicky dies knowing that "Polly would make a fine woman," and that she and Rudolf will stay on the land.

Later that summer Doctor Ed stops at Rosicky's grave, within sight of the homestead. Close by the wire fence is Rosicky's mowing machine. The boys had been cutting hay that afternoon, and "the new-cut hay perfumed all the night air" (70). Here is the undercurrent of time's "duration": the lovely blue-green alfalfa, recalled by Rosicky, led him to save the field here in the new world, to carry forward its beauty, its perfume. Rosicky was "a very simple man" like "a tree that has not many roots, but one tap-root that goes down deep" (32). His intuitions radiate from his family, to the communal patterns that bind humans together, and finally to vegetable life, to the very ground itself.

The rhetoric of this story is simple, unliterary; indeed, Rosicky's dialect ("Dat widder woman bring her daughter up very nice" [7]) skirts comic book idiom at times. Cather's accomplishment lies in conveying Rosicky's unspoken sensitivities, in giving voice to his sense of the unity of the human and natural world. Driving home from that first doctor's visit, Rosicky stops by the graveyard next to his fields to watch the first snow of autumn: ". . . a fine sight to see the snow falling so quietly and graciously over so much open country. On his cap and shoulders, on the horses' backs and manes, light, delicate, mysterious it fell; and with it a dry cool fragrance was released into the air" (19). Later in the year, walking home at night after doing Polly's dishes, Rosicky meditates—if that is the right word—even more explicitly on the simultaneity of two times, two loves, one near (his home) and one the encircling cosmos: "That kitchen with the shining windows was dear to him; but the sleeping fields and bright stars and the noble darkness were dearer still" (41). Stylistically, Cather has brought the two worlds together ("sleeping fields"; "noble darkness") joining the everyday objective world and the unfathomable other.

One aspect of "Neighbour Rosicky" is unique in Cather's work: her stress on patriotism through her pointed references to Independence Day. As a writer, Cather is singularly unconcerned with sociopolitical problems or contexts. Her interests are elsewhere, with the personal and, ultimately, the metaphysical. In this one story, however, she dwells on her version of the American dream—actually the original, Jeffersonian American dream of the yeoman farmer, independent and virtuous. Rosicky has been an American success, we might say, yet he wants for his sons not greater success but goodness and the freedom of personal action. He wants to perpetuate the possibility of virtuous living. As Cather well knew, the American dream had been thoroughly tarnished; in thus reasserting its oldest lineaments, she was recreating an early America of the imagination.

"Old Mrs. Harris"

"Old Mrs. Harris," the second of the stories in *Obscure Destinies*, has come to be the most admired of the three, and Cather herself thought it her best. She must have felt that she had succeeded in catching something precious to her, for she scarcely bothers disguising the richly autobiographical detail.[48] Anyone visiting the old Cather home in Red Cloud (now restored and open to visitors) immediately recognizes the crowded little rooms of the Templeton house.

The large Templeton family itself is the focus of the story, in particular the grandmother, the Mrs. Harris of the title; her daughter, Victoria; and her fifteen-year-old granddaughter, called Vickie (as Willa was called Willie in her family). Vickie, ambitious and intent on making her own way, is impatient with family claims, though she likes to read stories to her young brothers. The household also includes Mandy, a "bound girl," who resembles a simple young woman who came with the Cather family from Virginia and lived with them throughout her life. Neighbors of the Templetons, Mr. and Mrs. Rosen, are drawn from the real-life Wieners, German Jews educated in the European fashion, who loaned the young Cather books from their extensive library. The story makes us sense the pleasure Cather takes in sheer remembering. Her style is expansive and unhurried, seeming to have room for everyone in the family and in the town itself.

The town, called Skyline, Colorado, is more than a backdrop. We need to feel its ethos to understand the Templetons and the Rosens, neither of whom fit easily into the town's fabric—the Templetons because they are Southerners, with ancestral roots in Tennessee, and the Rosens because they are from a larger, cosmopolitan world.

The town prides itself on its firm standards in ethics and deportment. It is a "snappy little Western democracy," with egalitarian notions about each person's due (*OD*, 133). Not that the town lacks a hierarchy: the poor Maude children, who may have different fathers, stand outside the fence at the ice cream social until Mrs. Templeton invites them in; a Mexican with a cart and two mules hauls away tin cans and refuse. The businessmen are "hard money grubbers," different from boyish Hillary Templeton, who refuses to call in loans when times are hard, or from Mr. Rosen, who has leisurely lunches away from his clothing store. Disagreeable Mrs. Jackson, another Templeton neighbor, appears to act for the town when she deliberately insults Victoria Templeton at the ice cream social, letting her know that her neglect of her mother, Grandma Harris, has been observed and condemned. Mrs. Harris, not Victoria, made the cake the Templetons brought, and Mrs. Jackson sniffs that she would never keep someone in her kitchen to bake for her. Only gradually does the hurt sink in.

For Victoria, it was "another of those thrusts . . . she couldn't understand" (128).

In truth, Victoria's treatment of her mother has bothered Mrs. Rosen, too. To outer eyes, Grandma Harris occupies a position in the Templeton family little above that of Mandy. Mrs. Harris gets up early to give breakfast to the children, then serves Victoria and Mr. Templeton in the dining room. Her "room" is not a room at all, but a passageway from kitchen to dining room, cluttered with the children's rocking horse and the clothing they throw off as they rush by. Her calico dresses and the tobacco box holding her soap are behind a cloth curtain in one corner.

Gradually we learn the nature of the position Mrs. Harris occupies in this family. It is understandable only against a Southern "feudal society" (133), of which Mrs. Harris is a remnant. Keeping her handsome daughter a "belle," and then the properly treated mistress of the house (so different from being a mere housekeeper), is the last mark of distinction she can preserve. To see Victoria a household drudge would have meant "real poverty, coming down in the world so far that one could no longer keep up appearances" (134). Mrs. Harris's sense of the fitness of things goes further than appearances, however. The one time she shows anger is in defense of proper burial for Blue Boy, the family cat. This time she defies Victoria, who would have Blue Boy taken away as trash, and tells the little boys to get up early and bury him in a little grave next to the sand creek. In protection of the right way to behave Mrs. Harris can be assertive, though for herself she is undemanding.

Grandma Harris must be understood in the context of the world of the old South; she finds her identity within the group, formerly a big kinship and surrounding community, now shrunk to her daughter and her family. But when the old forms are sufficiently kept, she feels content—indeed, happy. Aging, becoming ever less an individual, a personality, Mrs. Harris attains a kind of animal dignity ("There was the kind of nobility about her head that there is about an old lion's: an absence of self-consciousness, vanity, preoccupation—something absolute" [81]).

Despite her passive acceptance of what life has offered, Mrs. Harris, like Rosicky, acts out of a deep wisdom to protect the future. When Vickie wins a scholarship through hard competition, but finds that she still needs three hundred dollars to finance her first year of college, her father weakly hopes she will postpone her plans, and her mother fails to understand her distress; she thinks tears appropriate only for a broken romance. Unknown to all, even to Vickie, proud Mrs. Harris secretly asks the Rosens to grant Vickie the necessary loan.

The story moves toward simultaneous but individual crises in the lives of the three Templeton women, as if to illustrate a truth about family living that Cather had found in the stories of Katherine Mansfield: "every individual in that household (even the children) is clinging passionately to his individual soul, is in terror of losing it in the general family flavour" (*OW*, 108–9). Vickie, having gotten her loan, thinks only of preparing to leave, and of all her needs. Victoria, in despair at finding that she is pregnant for the sixth time, locks her bedroom door. "She was sick of it all; sick of dragging this chain of life that never let her rest" (178). And old Mrs. Harris is dying. As she rests on her narrow cot she is ministered to by one of the ten-year-old twins, who spreads his own handkerchief on a box for a bedside table, brings fresh water in a real glass tumbler, and reads *Joe's Luck* to her. "Grandmother was perfectly happy" (184).

When the family learns just how ill Grandma Harris is, they begin to fuss, as Grandma had known and feared they would. The doctor is called, and Mrs. Harris is lifted from her cot and put in Victoria's bed, dressed in one of Victoria's nice nightgowns. Of all this Mrs. Harris knows nothing; she had received the appropriate attentions from her young grandson.

A remarkable paragraph closes the story. Abruptly the narrative voice moves us to a distant future time, leaving us disoriented, caught in an *aporia* between two perspectives. It is an old narrative device, but also modern, in its disquieting refusal of closure:

> Thus Mrs. Harris slipped out of the Templetons' story; but Victoria and Vickie had still to go on, to follow the long road that leads through things unguessed at and unforeseeable. When they are old, they will come closer and closer to Grandma Harris. They will think a great deal about her, and remember things they never noticed; and their lot will be more or less like hers.

How can intense young Vickie or touchy Victoria be like self-effacing Mrs. Harris? How can "their lot" resemble hers? Only the mysteriously beneficent dissolutions of time hold the answer.

"Old Mrs. Harris" tells us much about Cather's deepest, most abiding themes and loves, among them her desire for learning, for the larger sphere of knowledge that high culture confers. Though young Vickie's intensity is handled with gentle satire, her aspiration is not. She yearns to have the breadth of understanding of Mr. Rosen, who "carried a country of his own in his mind, and was able to unfold it like a tent in any wilderness" (121).

"Old Mrs. Harris" responds to a variety of approaches. Obviously there is much to engage the biographer and the student of social history. Feminist historians and critics find scenes relevant to the position of women at that time: Grandma Harris, trying to find the three hundred dollars Vickie needs for her education, first approaches her son-in-law, who sold Mrs. Harris's old home in Tennessee. She finds that the funds are invested and safe, but not available ("Invested; that was a word men always held over women, Mrs. Harris thought, and it always meant they could have none of their own money" [165]). Other scenes speak to questions of gender. Victoria's sense of entrapment at becoming pregnant again is fully voiced: "She had had babies enough; and there ought to be an end to such apprehensions some time before you were old and ugly" (178). Yet this scene must be placed against an earlier one, her loving pleasure in nursing the last baby, beautiful little Hughie (115). Cather writes with a deep appreciation of woman's paradoxical biological destiny. In fact, it is hard to leave off thinking about "Old Mrs. Harris," so rich and teasing are its many facets.

"Two Friends"

The young Cather is also a character, a listener, in "Two Friends," the last of the three *Obscure Destinies* stories—doubly a presence, for the narrator is the youth grown up, now experienced, one who has traveled in "Southern countries" yet remembers the breach that she saw growing between two friends as "an old scar" (229–30). True, the narrator remains nameless—in fact, genderless—but it is impossible not to hear Cather's own voice. Further, the two friends of the story are recognizable as two men prominent in the Red Cloud of Cather's girlhood. When "Two Friends" was published, Cather wrote to her old friend Carrie Miner, whose father served as the model for Mr. Dillon, hoping that Carrie will find the portrait acceptable. She adds that in any case she was not attempting to portray the men exactly; rather something they suggested.[49]

What they suggest is friendship, an affectional bond little explored in modern literature, though it engaged classical thinkers, as Cather would have known. One may fancy that she was remembering Aristotle's discussion of friendship, or Cicero's, and was testing their ideas in a little town in the New World. The quality of this story is meditative throughout. The narrative voice begins with an observation in the tone of a moral philosopher, speculating on a basic human need: "Even in early youth, when the mind is so eager for the new and untried, while it is still a stranger to faltering and fear, we yet like to think that there are certain unalterable realities, somewhere at the bottom of things" (*OD*, 193). This opening contrasts decidedly with the way the other two stories begin, where we are immediately in the middle of some personal worry. The mutual regard between friends is calmer, steadier, than the intricate loves within families, with their hurts and emotional intensities. Indeed, the friendship between Mr. Dillon and Mr. Trueman is markedly set apart from family. When Mr. Dillon, married and with children, goes home after their evening talks, Mr. Trueman, a widower, takes up his own private life, usually playing poker with gambling cronies. Free of the entangling needs and responsibilities of family life, the bond of friendship should be one of the "unalterable realities . . . at the bottom of things." When this proves not the case, it leaves a "scar" on the developing soul of the young girl that she takes with her all her days, a reminder of all the uncertainties of a world in which change is the principle.

The friendship is important to the girl not only for the solidity it represents, but because the two men, in their talk and deportment, explain and enlarge her world. From their secure vantage points—town banker and store owner (Mr. Dillon) and cattleman (Mr. Trueman)—they transmit to the listening girl what a community should provide its young: accurate knowledge about the world and the wisdom of experience. She is educated by "the old stories of the early West . . . ; the minute biographies of the farming people; the clear, detailed, illuminating accounts of all that went on in the great crop-growing, cattle-feeding world; and the silence—the strong, rich, out-flowing silence between two friends" (226). She hears ethical judgments. Mr. Dillon defends the Swedish farmers who work their women hard ("It's the old-country way; they're accustomed to it, and they like it"), but Mr. Trueman does not acquiesce ("Maybe. I don't like it" [204]). She learns, too, about the world outside Singleton, Kansas, as the men talk of St. Joseph, of Chicago. Their journeys "made the rest of us feel less shut away and small-townish" (202). She observes the forebearance and trust that make friendship possible. Mr. Dillon curbs his tendency to sharp opinions in Mr. Trueman's presence; Mr. Trueman cautions only quietly against quack social cures ("Mustn't be a reformer, R. E. Nothing in it" [214]).

One particular moment in this delicate relationship—two busy men, a quiet girl—is held for us, crystallizing its dynamics. On a hot summer night, with the dusty street before them "drinking up the moonlight," the three are in their accustomed places. The two men sit and talk, and the girl listens. That night they observe an occultation of Venus. As they watch, the planet appears to move toward the moon, to be swallowed, and then to appear on the other side. The scene is a tableau: the three watching figures; the intense moonlight making the deep dust of the street silvery; the dust that—so the narrative voice tells us—is one of the possible answers, one of the "unalterable realities" ("the last residuum of material things—the soft bottom resting place"); and above the scene, the mysterious heavenly bodies, a cosmos enclosing all. The narrator stops the moment by drawing the scene in painterly fashion, suggesting forms by spots of color. Rickety wooden buildings across the street become "an immaterial structure of velvet-white and glossy blackness, with here and there a faint smear of blue door, or a tilted patch of sage-green." The brick wall behind the two men "took on a carnelian hue" and the shadows of the men "made two dark masses on the white sidewalk" (210–11).[50] One is reminded of another writer's attempt to recreate a lost moment: Woolf's Lily Briscoe, as she tries to recapture her memory of Mrs. Ramsey in paint.

But the pattern of the story is of movement and change, unsettling—not just the eclipse of Venus, which prefigures the end of the friendship, but the swiftness with which it happens, when "everything up there overhead seemed as usual" (212).

This is not the first time that we have noted Cather using the night sky as a manifest for lurking questions. In "The Enchanted Bluff," for example, one of the boys says that the North Star may not last forever, and in "Before Breakfast" Venus seems to radiate reassurances to the irritable Grenfell. Like the mad farmer in Frost's "The Star-Splitter," characters in these stories turn to the sky for clues. In "Two Friends" what the sky patterns reveal—whether they reveal—is left as a question.

After talk of the eclipse, Mr. Dillon turns impatiently to practical worries, how to get tramps off the railroad or rid the town of one fancy house at least. Mr. Trueman, in contrast, hopes that the cosmos is a coherent one: "Maybe the stars will throw some light on all that, if we get the run of them" (214).

By chance, a surviving letter of Cather's reveals just how personal a wondering contemplation of the heavens was for her. From her letter it is clear that Mr. Trueman and Frost's star-splitter are figures whose hope for transcendence she shared. Writing to Edith Lewis from Jaffrey, New Hampshire, Cather tells of watching Venus and Jupiter in the evening sky for an hour, and questioning whether the movement of these bodies may not signal something more than physical and mathematical forces.[51]

Yet what ends the friendship is not a stroke of fate—at least not apparently. Rather it is a human failing, a burst of ego. Mr. Dillon's irritable temperament breaks through his imperfectly acquired habit of patience. Though the narrator throughout the story treats the men as equals, speaking with mild irony of "my heroes" or "my two great men," it is clear that Mr. Dillon is the lesser man. He is more intelligent, the narrator says; that is, he knows precise commercial values: the worth of the Swede farmers, the mortgage of the homesteader who foolishly has a traveling photographer take a picture of his house and barn, the unacceptable risk of granting a loan to a "foolish, extravagant woman or a girl he didn't approve of," when the tone of his voice, "though courteous," was "relentless as the multiplication table" (207). A man of strong prejudices, a good Catholic and family man, Mr. Dillon had curbed his dislike of poker playing, of questionable women, of Republicanism (all habits and interests of Trueman) out of respect for his friend. But on a trip to Chicago Dillon hears Bryan's inflaming "cross of gold" speech, and it unleashes his temper and local partisanship. He sacrifices Trueman's friendship.

In contrast, Trueman (the name suggestive), slow of speech, moves in a world singularly free of calculation: he keeps one–hundred–dollar bills in his pocket, but leaves his coat hanging in cattle sheds or the barber shop; when he changes banks, he does not know the figure of his account, but writes a check for "the amount of my balance." More, his generosity is of the spirit ("one felt solidity, an entire absence of anything mean or small" [196]). A magnanimous man, large-souled, he walks "spaciously, as if he were used to a great deal of room" (203). There is something antique about Trueman, indeed heroic; he moves as though "on the deck of his own ship" (214) and the ring he wears is "the head of a Roman soldier cut in onyx" (199). Unlike Dillon,

Trueman knows the worth of friendship. When Dillon dies suddenly of pneumonia, Trueman gives the young girl a red seal from his watch chain "as a keepsake," and moves away from Singleton. We are told that he dies in San Francisco, where the trail leading West must end. And it is Trueman who tells us what our stance should be toward the mysterious chances that beset us. One of the pleasures of the young observer is hearing her two friends talk of theatrical performances and actors and actresses. Trueman remembers Edwin Booth in *Richard II*, "which made a great impression on me at the time." But now, he says, "that play's a little too tragic. Something very black about it. I think I prefer *Hamlet*" (217). This must be our clue—not the anguish and regret of Richard, but the readiness of Hamlet, the acceptance of a universe where change, and so loss, is one of the unalterable realities.

A hint of transcendence remains. The great natural world of the stars and planets confers an inspiriting beauty on all that lies below; the materialism of the dust may not be the full answer. The silvery glow that moonlight casts on the soft dust of the town's streets, making it lovely, beautifying it, suggests that an ultimate harmony is the answer. "Nothing in the world, not snow mountains or blue seas, is so beautiful in moonlight as the soft, dry summer roads in a farming country, roads where the white dust falls back from the slow wagon-wheel" (212).

The title Cather selected for her three stories, taken from Gray's elegy ("Let not Ambition mock their useful toil, / Their homely joy, and destiny obscure"), fits her collection well enough, but Cather's attitude toward her material carries nothing of Gray's sentimental condescension—no flower "wastes its sweetness on the desert air" here. Missing also are the grotesqueries of Anderson's Winesburg and the boorishness of Lewis's Gopher Prairie. What one carries away from reading *Obscure Destinies* is a sense of lives lived in full humanity. The West of Cather's imagination had not always allowed this scope, as a glance back at the small towns in, for example, "The Sculptor's Funeral" or "The Joy of Nelly Deane" reminds us.

"Like those Nicèan barks of yore": *The Old Beauty and Others*

Following Cather's death in 1947, Edith Lewis, named by Cather her literary executor, and Alfred Knopf, her publisher since 1920, brought out *The Old Beauty and Others*, three stories Cather left in manuscript. The first, "The Old Beauty," was written in 1936; "The Best Years" and "Before Breakfast" only shortly before her death. As it happens, the three have very different settings. "Before Breakfast" (discussed in chapter 1) takes place on Grand Manan, and Cather's love for the silences and vistas of this northern island, where she had a summer home, is palpable; "The Best Years" is her last obeisance to the Nebraska of her memories; and "The Old Beauty" is set in the south of France, in the resort town of Aix-les-Bains. Recalling Cather's pleasure in the French landscape she first saw in 1902, so vivid in the travel pieces she wrote then, we might say that these stories make a farewell gesture toward three of the spots Cather loved best on "the green surface where men lived and trees lived and blue flags and buttercups" (*OB*, 161).

Taken together, the three comprise a final expression of Cather's particular quality. Only, perhaps, with "The Best Years" do we sense a slackening into self-indulgence. The grim Divide of Cather's early Nebraska stories is missing, replaced by calendar scenes ("Big red barns, rows of yellow straw stacks, green orchards, trim white farmhouses, fenced gardens" [80]), and the landscape feels dimmed into an idea ("The horizon was like a perfect circle, a great embrace, and within it lay the cornfields, still green, and the yellow wheat stubble, miles and miles of it, and the pasture lands where the white-faced cattle led lives of utter content" [78]). True, the human world is not so easily content. The great embrace must encompass human loss—a poignant one, the death of the bright young teacher Leslie Ferguesson. The pain of loss is still an emotional hurt long after her death, though now some of Leslie's pupils are themselves teachers, passing on to yet another generation, we assume, some of Leslie's delicacy of feeling.

The story is done in delicate pastels, rather like the tonal qualities of Cather's penultimate novel, *Lucy Gayheart,* which also tells of the death of a vibrant young woman.

One little passage in "The Best Years" carries a hint of a mystery at the heart—a doubleness in memory, something beyond personal continuity. When Evangeline Knightly, the county superintendent, visits Leslie's little school, she "made a joking little talk to the children and told them about a very bright little girl in Scotland who knew nearly a whole play of Shakespeare's by heart, but who wrote in her diary: "Nine times nine is the Devil"; which proved, she said, that there are two kinds of memory, and God is very good to anyone to whom he gives both kinds" (86–87). We are not told what the pupils in advanced arithmetic thought of this odd "joke." In darkling fashion, Cather may be inserting herself, the artist, into this simple story, addressing us directly to remind us that without those who, by a gift, see beneath simple figures into other forces (demons, trolls, goblins), personal memory, however loving, would dim into impotence.

This hint at the need for double sight might have been inserted with greater appropriateness, I feel, in "The Old Beauty." It makes greater demands on attentiveness than is usual for a Cather story, and as a consequence is generally underrated. Readers typically find Gabrielle Longstreet, an aging beauty left over from the Victorian age, an unlikely Cather heroine and her story disappointing. In fact, its very first reader, the editor of the *Woman's Home Companion,* where Cather sent it in 1936, felt this way. She agreed to print the story, even as she said she did not like it, but Cather withdrew the manuscript. Biographers and critics often pass over "The Old Beauty" with some embarrassment. One appears to speak for most in calling it "the somewhat querulous writing of old age."[52]

The chief stumbling block is the central character, Gabrielle Longstreet. Once a celebrated international beauty, she is now, in 1922, a "ruin"; further, she is difficult and forbidding in manner—she sees nothing in the world forming after World War I that pleases her ("I think one should go out with one's time" [46]). The question has to be, How did Cather, at age sixty-three still writing brilliantly (if nothing else, the rhetorical chiaroscuro of her last novel, *Sapphira and the Slave Girl,* shows her powers intact)—how did she think of Gabrielle Longstreet?

Part 1

The faded spa world of Aix-les-Bains is a suitable background for Gabrielle. Though the town is not vividly present, Cather knew it well. She had first seen it in 1923, and in 1930 she had stayed in a resort hotel much like the Hôtel Splendide. She admired its square and gardens, and especially its air of having survived unchanged from an older time. During her 1930 visit she had an encounter that may have prompted her imagination to play over the situation of living beyond one's time. Staying at the hotel was a distinguished elderly woman who, Cather learned in conversation, was Flaubert's niece—someone who had known intimately this great master, as Cather thought of him, and others, such as Turgenev.

Cather wrote a short essay, "A Chance Meeting," about this occasion, and she included it in a collection of her literary essays, called *Not under Forty*, that she was assembling in 1936 while also working on "The Old Beauty."

However, this real-life encounter provides no more than the faintest outline of "The Old Beauty." Lady Longstreet is quite unlike the vigorous Mme. Grout, as she is unlike the fictional portraits of age—Rosicky, for example, or Mrs. Harris—that Cather had recently composed. We have to look elsewhere for the true lineaments of the story.

"The Old Beauty" is told through the eyes of an American businessman, Henry Seabury, who had been one of Gabrielle's admirers when he was young and she was a reigning beauty. In the opening scene Seabury is approached by reporters outside the Hôtel Splendide. They have just learned that the celebrated Lady Longstreet, who had been registered under another name, has died here the night before. Seabury refuses to help them with their story, but as he watches the litter bearing Gabrielle's body leave the hotel, he realizes that there is no one waiting for the news. Gabrielle has left no family or intimates, and though no doubt remembered by men like himself "scattered about the world," men who had worshiped her beauty, she has been largely forgotten. Were beauties such as she had been, then, "illusions" (25)? This becomes the question of the story. Searching for an answer, Seabury recalls the past two months here at the hotel after he recognized Gabrielle—teas, excursions, and drives, including the disastrous trip into the mountains the day before she died—and also scenes from Gabrielle at the height of her fame.

These are the "events" of the story. As it ends, Seabury is at the railway station seeing the coffin put on the express that will bear it to

Paris and its place in the cemetery of Père-Lachaise. Gabrielle will rest there, the final line of the story tells us, with "Adelina Patti, Sarah Bernhardt, and other ladies who had once held a place in the world" (72).[53]

Here we have the puzzle of the story, Seabury's question in a slightly different form: Does Gabrielle Longstreet merit lying next to Patti and Bernhardt—next to two of the greatest artists of their time? Cather had long ago answered this question with a firm no. In the opinionated arts and theater reviews she wrote for the Nebraska papers while a student, Lily Langtry, then at the height of her fame and notoriety, serves as the exemplar of the actress with looks but no talent that the principled Cather deplored. At the time of the Langtry divorce, then a scandalous event, Cather wrote, "Another instance of the short mutable reigns of these women who travel only on their beauty and wardrobes and unenviable reputations is the inglorious fall of Lillie Langtry." And "this woman," the pitiless young voice continues, "was called a genius by an infatuated rabble."[54] More significantly, a column of 1897 actually links the three names of Patti, Bernhardt, and Langtry. Cather is scolding a New York impresario for sponsoring Langtry ("the most brazen sham, the 'Jersey Lily' . . . the idol of the London 'chappies'") along with Patti ("the most glorious voice in the world") and Sarah Bernhardt ("the greatest artist in the world").[55]

But the most telling item among these early pieces is a little anecdote Cather uses to open a column. It is Seabury's question in embryo: Is service to this beauty service to an illusion?

> A little while ago a man who had once, years ago, saved Langtry's life, was found dead. In his vest pocket was found Langtry's card, so worn that it was almost illegible. These are the materials for a story if you care to write it. Langtry is neither good nor great, but this poor devil probably went through life with the sublime conviction that he had saved an angel and an artist unaware.[56]

These "materials for a story" were transformed by forty years of thinking and observing before emerging into "The Old Beauty." The question that is asked is the ancient one, what is the connection of beauty to goodness or greatness?

From these columns, too, we learn what an honor Cather pays Gabrielle in putting her to rest in Père-Lachaise. Even before Cather visited the cemetery in 1902, her romantic imagination had seen it as "that burial ground of genius,"[57] full of the "mighty graves"[58] of those like Balzac or Chopin, known by a single name.

In short, Cather's early journalism tells us that "The Old Beauty," seemingly so uncharacteristic put next to the great Nebraska stories of *Obscure Destinies*, is yet about persons and questions that had lingered in her mind. The voice of "The Old Beauty" is not the sudden crankiness of old age. With its long gestation, the story fulfills a definition of literature Sarah Orne Jewett once gave Cather, and that she was fond of quoting: "The thing that teases the mind over and over for years, and at last gets itself put down rightly on paper—whether little or great, it belongs to Literature."[59]

Given her interest in Langtry, however condescending, and her liking for memoirs and biographies (except for her own) it is highly likely that Cather read Langtry's autobiography, *The Days I Knew*, when it came out in 1925, with a preface by the actor Richard LeGallienne. Something LeGallienne said may have struck her. In any case he articulates a perspective that Cather seems to adopt in her story: "Of all forms of fame that of Beauty is the greatest, in that it is the simplest, for it is not the fame of achievement, . . . but of a miracle. . . . such fame has been Mrs. Langtry's all her days."[60]

Cather clearly had the facts of Langtry's life in mind as she created Gabrielle, for the resemblances are many: both Lily and Gabrielle were born on an island (Lily on Jersey, Gabrielle on Martinique); both were fluent in English and French; both married English yachtsmen who took them to ancestral homes in the north of England and then to London, where their beauty instantly won them a place in the highest society. Both went through a divorce and had shadowy second husbands. Lily loved horses and kept a racing stable; English visitors in Aix-les-Bains recall seeing Gabrielle riding in Devonshire before the war. Lily wore her hair in the "Langtry knot"; Gabrielle wore hers in the "mode Gabrielle" (18). Lily liked to travel with photographs of former friends and admirers; one of the significant scenes in "The Old Beauty" is Seabury's introduction to Gabrielle's gallery. "We carry so many photographs about with us, Mr. Seabury," explains Cherry Beamish, the former music hall actress who is Gabrielle's companion.[61] Cather does not give Gabrielle a stage career; she leaves her a famous beauty only.

To read *The Days I Knew* is to be struck with a further parallel, one of greater significance than a matter of style or career. As Langtry's account of her life goes on, one cannot escape the impression of dreadful blandness, an emptiness at the center. Langtry tells of encounters with the great and notable of two generations—the highest royalty, of course, but also men of affairs (Gladstone, Disraeli, President Grant, Rothschild), great actresses (Sarah Bernhardt, Ellen Terry), and always artists and writers. Oscar Wilde was devoted, lying all night at her doorstep, bringing her a single amaryllis, writing a poem for her, "To Helen, formerly of Troy, now of London." "Jimmy" Whistler painted her, and she knew, or met, Ruskin, Kipling, Rosetti, Swinburne, Burne-Jones, William Morris. But one hopes in vain for telling glimpses of these figures. The pictures Langtry gives are perfunctory, or cold: the devoted Wilde had "pale freckles" and "greenish-hued teeth" (Langtry, 83). The great figures of her time flicker through her pages like so many ghosts.

As Seabury escorts Gabrielle and Cherry about, we learn that one of Gabrielle's chief concerns is that she had been, like Langtry, "indifferent" in the days of her beauty. She had supposed that "a great man's time, his consideration, his affection, were mine in the natural course of things" (33). Now, aged, her beauty gone, she "suffers from strange regrets" (43). She fears she was "cold" to her friends (43), and now she is trying really to know them. "I read everything they wrote, and everything that has been written about them. That is my chief pleasure. . . . They are dearer to me than when they were my living friends" (33–34). It is as though she is trying to live her life over, correcting its mistakes.

Is her memory accurate? Had she been "cold"? Seabury recalls her "calm grey eyes" and "calm white shoulders." Her eyes had "no sparkle" in them, but rather a "kind of twilight shadow" (24). She was "flowerlike," and her London rooms were rather "cool and spring-like" (helped by a rare hot-air furnace). She had not been witty or clever; she said "nothing memorable" in either French or English (17). She was not a coquette; she seemed "unconscious of her body and whatever clothed it," and her hands lay on her dress forgotten, "as a bunch of white violets might lie" (24). She had "the air of having come from afar off" (24). She did not attract would-be lovers, but rather a series of Great Protectors. The remarkable men around her were either old or young, as Seabury had been, not men her own age.

Seabury recalls one incident of some dramatic tension, a genteel rescue. Calling to take her to dinner, he entered her drawing room to find her struggling against a stout, dark man who has her pinioned on the sofa, one hand thrust in her bodice. The man rushes out, and Gabrielle slowly recovers. Only in this instance, she tells Seabury years later, did a man mistake her manner for sexual invitation.

Despite the absence of the erotic in Gabrielle's appeal, Seabury hesitates to call her cold; rather, he says, she was "unawakened" (he uses the word twice [18, 44]). Hers was a beauty for contemplation, not possession. It gave refreshment to women as well as men. "Wasn't she the most beautiful creature then!" recalls Cherry. "I used to see her at the races, and at charity balls" (44). Mrs. Thompson, the Englishwoman who first identifies the gaunt old woman to Seabury as Lady Longstreet, mourns the passing of "those beautiful ones. . . . We never have too many of them" (14).

Gradually we perceive that Gabrielle, not at home in the postwar era, was not at home in her own time either. She had "never dressed in the mode" (18). When she talked to the older men who visited her, she asked them "about events and personages already in the past; things she had come too late to see" (19). As her mythic form takes shape, filling in Gabrielle's outline, we see her as indeed coming "from afar." As Wilde's poem would have it, she was once of Troy. She was simply Beauty (ancient beauty, the idea of beauty) temporally embodied.

Now, with her beauty gone, something like a real self is struggling to be born. Seabury reflects, "in this world people have to pay an extortionate price for any exceptional gift whatever" (15). He sees that Gabrielle is trying (without success) to recapture the life that should have been hers.

Cather frequently expressed her belief that the life given to art demands the sacrifice of personal life. The face of Eden Bower, on the way to sing the role of Aphrodite, is hard and masklike, and the singer Thea Kronborg, in *The Song of the Lark*, says that her work has become her life. Gabrielle is a poignant instance of this deprivation in that her peculiar gift, simple beauty, has demanded no awareness, no passionate desire, no fires of youth to burn into art. This is the explanation for Gabrielle's rigidity, her inability to adapt or change. An icon for most of her term on earth, she has no memory of having lived. Only those engaged with life (Rosicky, Mrs. Harris) know how to respond. Gabrielle's tragedy (not too strong a word) is that no vestige of a self exists for her to recover.

Gabrielle's doomed search ends during a trip into the mountains on the last day of her life. Seabury has hired a car for a drive up to Grande Chartreuse, a medieval Carthusian monastery. As the climb goes on, it begins to seem a journey into another world. "Ever afterward Seabury remembered that drive as strangely impersonal. . . . The lightness and purity of the air gave one a sense of detachment from everything one had left behind 'down there, back yonder' "(62). All gradually grow silent, even the young mountain boy who drives them. Dramatically, the quiet is broken once: "the gold tones of an alpine horn" float down, and the driver stops so that all can listen to this eerie, disembodied trumpet. It seems meant for Gabrielle. The monastery itself, dwarfed by crags, is "superb and solitary." Seabury has the sense that "life would go on thus forever in high places, among naked peaks cut sharp against a stainless sky" (62).

This operatic preparation sets the scene for some decisive moment, some revelation. But no vision is granted. Hugh Kenner, writing of the narrative pattern of Joyce's stories, speaks of "disappointed epiphanies."[62] It is such a blank that we experience here—the journey taken, the destination reached, and then nothing.

Seabury and Cherry go into the monastery; Gabrielle remains behind, looking into a great well at the center of the cobblestoned courtyard. A lone woman at an ancient well, the immensity of nature behind her—it is a richly allusive image, like a painting in the manner of the picturesque sublime. Our attention is held, rather as it is held by the painterly portrayal of the three watching figures in "Two Friends."

Gabrielle takes a little mirror from her handbag and throws a beam of light into the water below, as though looking more deeply, trying to get to the bottom of things. At first, we are told, "that yellow ray seemed to waken the black water at the bottom: little ripples stirred over the surface," and Gabrielle "smiled as she threw the gold plaque over the water" (64). Later she is "still looking down into the well and playing with her little reflector, a faintly contemptuous smile on her lips" (64). Why "contemptuous"? Does she perceive the futility of her search for instant selfhood? And are we meant to notice items in the scene that she cannot read—the "gold plaque" awakening "the black water" as an image of beauty and art (the mirror held to nature) enlightening, enhancing, a dark world?

At a minimum, the figure at the well represents a moment of searching wonder. Possibly Cather recalls Robert Frost's use of this same picture of frustrated hope. Like Gabrielle, his well gazer at first sees a vague form; then

> . . . a ripple
> Shook whatever it was lay there at bottom,
> Blurred it, blotted it out. What was that whiteness?
> Truth? A pebble of quartz? For once, then, something.[63]

Gabrielle too sees "ripples" that blur into ambiguity, or nothingness.

On the trip down the mountain the car with Gabrielle, Cherry, and Seabury meets with an accident that, although not serious in itself, leads to Gabrielle's death in her sleep that night. Seemingly unharmed by the jolt, Gabrielle is unduly upset—irrationally repulsed—by the two young women driving the car that caused the accident. They are rough beasts indeed (whatever their ultimate destination)—American girls, smoking, wearing white breeches. A new dispensation has arrived, and Gabrielle's day is done.

Yet Gabrielle's death may not be the seal to personal failure and frustration. It may be that the vision denied Gabrielle at the well visited her as death approached in the night. The next morning, as Cherry and Seabury view her corpse, they note that she had put on her rings, and that they are on hands that look strangely young again. Her face is "regal, calm, victorious—like an open confession" (70). The startling word *confession*, with its archaic overtones, points to public avowal, to self-definition and assertion, rather than to an acknowledgment of guilt. At the moment of death, it is hinted, Gabrielle understood who she was; was proud of how she had served. Cather does not tell us the source of this understanding, or where Gabrielle came from: Plato's realm of the imperishable, perhaps, or, a not-unrelated spot, the home of Poe's Helen, "the regions which / Are Holy-Land!" Looking at those youthful hands and that victorious face, Seabury must have had his answer—he had not remembered an illusion, but the truest reality.

The story tells us that Gabrielle does indeed deserve her place among the marbles of Père-Lachaise with the two great artists. She had faithfully carried her gift, her beauty, sacrificing the life of the self. "The Old Beauty" is Cather's belated apology to Lily Langtry.

That Cather had long pondered this theme, beauty as a gift to the world, is clear from a much earlier story. In "Jack-a-Boy," which appeared in the *Saturday Evening Post* in 1901, the bearer of the gift is a six-year-old-boy. He has soft blue-gray eyes, like Gabrielle's, and he too is associated with flowers, especially violets—he delivers May baskets to the aging inhabitants of a set of studio apartments. Unlike Gabrielle, he is a source of immediate moral harmony among the residents, and they explicitly recognize his unworldly quality. In this earlier story, the possible source, or home, of beauty as essence is debated. The old professor of Greek knows that "sometimes the old divinities reveal themselves in children" (*CSF*, 320). After Jack-a-Boy's early death from scarlet fever, the music teacher wonders whether the boy "heard the pipes of Pan as the old wood gods trooped by" (320), and a third resident, the narrator, thinks of the Christian incarnation. But the Greek professor appears to speak for all when he observes, "Perhaps Pater was right, and it is the revelation of beauty which is to be our redemption, after all" (322).

All three of Cather's last, posthumously published stories have common threads, despite their varying times, places, and situations. Gabrielle's beauty lingers in the minds of all who knew her; Venus, in stellar and clamshell form, invigorates Grenfell; and the memory of young Leslie Ferguesson remains a vital force. Central to all three is a desire for completeness—Gabrielle's restless queries, Grenfell's claim of self-sufficiency, Leslie's homesickness. Though frustrated by the sweep of time, whether the simple generations of a family or the eons of geology, these desires carry their own reward.

It is pleasant, too, to speculate that Cather may have been gently explaining (and ridiculing) herself in one of the portraits. She seems to accent Gabrielle's sniffy attitude toward the modern world, and her stubborn adherence to old fashions and forms—opinions and manners that apparently were Cather's as she grew older.[64] It may be that she is writing a wryly humorous apologia. The one set apart by a gift, the artist, is paradoxically the one least engaged in life, the one who risks becoming rigid, irrelevant, old-fashioned. A chosen one, a Narcissus, may stay at the well seeking Being in a world of Becoming, trapped by having to use terms (styles, words) that will not hold still.

Cather's stories are—in addition to much else—a record of her long struggle to understand fully the vocation she chose so early and followed with such fidelity.

Notes to Part 1

1. *The Professor's House* (New York: Alfred A. Knopf, 1925), 101.
2. "Katherine Mansfield," in *Willa Cather on Writing: Critical Studies on Writing as an Art* (1949; Lincoln: University of Nebraska Press, 1988), 109. Essays from this collection are hereafter cited in the text as *OW*.
3. Elizabeth Shepley Sergeant, foreword to *Willa Cather: A Memoir* (1953; Lincoln: University of Nebraska Press, 1986), 2; hereafter cited in the text.
4. Both quotations are from an interview in the Philadelphia *Record*, 10 August 1913, in *Willa Cather in Person: Interviews, Speeches, and Letters*, ed., L. Brent Bohlke, (Lincoln: University of Nebraska Press, 1986), 10.
5. In her doctor phase, Cather affected masculine dress, chopped off her hair, and signed herself "William Cather, M.D." Biographers treat this episode in differing ways: some as a tomboyish affectation, a posture of rebellion made acceptable by Alcott's Jo March; others as evidence of gender uncertainty, a lesbian orientation underlying her decision not to marry.
6. "Annual Commencement Exercises of the Red Cloud Public Schools," Red Cloud *Chief*, 13 June 1891, quoted in Bohlke, xxii; the speech itself is reprinted in Bohlke, 141–43.
7. Edith Lewis, *Willa Cather Living* (New York: Alfred A. Knopf, 1953), 22; hereafter cited in the text.
8. The relation of the story to the Canfield family is discussed in Susan J. Rosowski, *The Voyage Perilous: Willa Cather's Romanticism* (Lincoln: University of Nebraska Press, 1986), 23–24 (hereafter cited in the text), and Mark J. Madigan, "Willa Cather and Dorothy Canfield Fisher: Rift, Reconciliation, and *One of Ours*," in *Cather Studies*, I, ed. Susan J. Rosowski (Lincoln: University of Nebraska Press, 1990), 115–29.
9. *The Kingdom of Art: Willa Cather's First Principles and Critical Statements 1893–1896*, ed. Bernice Slote (Lincoln: University of Nebraska Press, 1966), 17; hereafter cited in the text as *KA*.
10. *Nebraska State Journal*, 1 March 1896; reprinted in *KA*, 417.
11. Katherine Anne Porter, in John J. Murphy, ed., *Critical Essays on Willa Cather* (Boston: G. K. Hall, 1984), 31.
12. Quoted in William H. Pritchard, *Frost: A Literary Life Reconsidered* (New York: Oxford University Press, 1984), 80.
13. See, for example, Lawrance Thompson, *Robert Frost: The Early Years* (New York: Holt, 1966), 381 and passim; John F. Sears, "William James, Henri

Bergson, and the Poetics of Robert Frost," *New England Quarterly* 48 (September 1975): 341–61; Paul Douglass, *Bergson, Eliot, and American Literature* (Lexington: University Press of Kentucky, 1986); Donald M. Kartiganer, *The Fragile Thread: The Meaning of Form in Faulkner's Novels* (Amherst: University of Massachusetts Press, 1979); Frank Lentricchia, "On the Ideologies of Poetic Modernism, 1890–1913: The Example of William James," in *Reconstructing American Literary History*, ed. Sacvan Bercovitch (Cambridge: Harvard University Press, 1986), 220–49; Tom Quirk, *Bergson and American Culture: The Worlds of Willa Cather and Wallace Stevens* (Chapel Hill: University of North Carolina Press, 1990). This last important work appeared after my study was completed.

14. George Seibel, *New Colophon* 2, pt. 7 (1949): 202.

15. Letter of 12 September 1912. The Sergeant letters are held in the Pierpont Morgan Library; photocopies in the Clifton Waller Barrett Library, University of Virginia. Cather's will forbids direct quotation.

16. Preface to *Alexander's Bridge* (Boston: Houghton Mifflin, 1922), vii.

17. William James, *Psychology: Briefer Course* (1892; Cambridge: Harvard University Press, 1984), 150.

18. "The Bookkeeper's Wife," in *Uncle Valentine and Other Stories*, ed. Bernice Slote (Lincoln: University of Nebraska Press, 1973), 97. Stories from this collection are hereafter cited in the text as *UVOS*.

19. "Edgar Allan Poe," Lincoln *Courier*, 12 October 1895; reprinted in *KA*, 82.

20. "The Novel Démeublé," in *OW*, 41–42.

21. Speech at Bowdoin College, 13 May 1925, as reported in the *Christian Science Monitor*, 14 May 1925; reprinted in Bohlke, 156.

22. "An Institute of Modern Literature," proceedings of the Bowdoin Conference, 1926; reprinted in Bohlke, 164.

23. Interview, San Francisco *Chronicle*, 29 March 1931; reprinted in Bohlke, 110–11.

24. "The Enchanted Bluff," in *Willa Cather's Collected Short Fiction, 1892–1912*, rev. ed., ed. Virginia Faulkner (Lincoln: University of Nebraska Press, 1970), 70. Stories in this collection are hereafter cited in the text as *CSF*.

25. "Before Breakfast," in *The Old Beauty and Others* (1948; New York: Vintage Books, 1976), 147. Stories from this collection are hereafter cited in the text as *OBO*.

26. Henri Bergson, *Creative Evolution*, trans. Arthur Mitchell (1911; New York: Random House, 1944), 195.

27. See, for instance, James Woodress's introduction to Willa Cather, *The Troll Garden* (Lincoln: University of Nebraska Press, 1983), xvi–xvii; Marilyn Arnold, *Willa Cather's Short Fiction* (Athens: Ohio University Press, 1984), 43–45; Sharon O'Brien, *Willa Cather: The Emerging Voice* (New York: Oxford University Press, 1987), 271–75; and Rosowski, 19–23.

28. Personal letter, Willa Cather to John Phillipson, 15 March 1943, Willa Cather Historical Center, Red Cloud, Nebraska.

Part 1

29. "Paul's Case," in *The Troll Garden*, ed. Woodress. Stories in this collection are hereafter cited in the text as *TG*.
30. The Table of Revisions in the Woodress edition does not note this deletion.
31. David A. Carpenter, "Why Willa Cather Revised 'Paul's Case': The Work in Art and Those Sunday Afternoons," *American Literature* 59 (1987): 590–608.
32. Unaccountably, Sharon O'Brien, who is much concerned with maternal images in Cather's early fiction, does not discuss this destructive mother.
33. See Table of Revisions in the Woodress edition. Cather also toned down or omitted other passages that pointed to Merrick's success or escape: she changed "genius" to "man like Harvey," and omitted, for example, "Upon whatever he had come in contact with, he had left a beautiful record of the experience—a sort of ethereal signature; a scent, a sound and colour that was his own."
34. James Woodress, *Willa Cather: A Literary Life* (Lincoln: University of Nebraska Press, 1987), 288; hereafter cited in the text. Woodress is paraphrasing a letter to Ferris Greenslet, 6 September 1918.
35. "The Diamond Mine," in *Youth and the Bright Medusa* (1920; Vintage Books, 1975), 119. Stories from this collection are hereafter cited in the text as *YBM*.
36. E. K. Brown, *Willa Cather: A Critical Biography*, completed by Leon Edel (New York: Alfred A. Knopf, 1953), 331.
37. Mary Ellman, *Thinking about Women* (New York: Harcourt, 1968), 114.
38. Blanche H. Gelfant, "The Forgotten Reaping-Hook: Sex in *My Ántonia*," *American Literature* 43 (1971):61.
39. The question of Cather's lesbianism is much discussed in critical and biographical writing. See, for instance, O'Brien, part 1 and passim; Woodress, *Life*, 141–42; Helen Cather Southwick, "Willa Cather's Early Career: Origins of a Legend," *Western Pennsylvania Historical Magazine* 65 (April 1982): 85–98; and David Stouck, "Recent Cather Scholarship: A Review," *Literature and Belief* 8 (1988):120–23.
40. The magazine version, called "Coming, Eden Bower!," is reprinted in *UVOS*, 141–76; the variants are listed in the Appendix, 177–81.
41. Not all commentators see Hedger and Eden following equal paths; rather, they see Hedger's as the true one and Eden's as false. See, for example, Thomas A. Gullason, "The 'Lesser' Renaissance: The American Short Story in the 1920s," in *The American Short Story 1900–1945* (Boston: Twayne, 1984), 58.
42. For explorations of Cather's religious views see the Willa Cather issue of *Literature and Belief* 8 (1988), especially the foreword by John J. Murphy and "Cather and Religion" by Mildred R. Bennett.

76

43. See, for instance, Arnold, 119–26; Bernice Slote, introduction to *UVOS*, xxiii–xxx; and Woodress, 359–61.

44. *Nebraska State Journal*, 24 March 1901; reprinted in *The World and the Parish: Willa Cather's Articles and Reviews, 1893–1902*, ed. William J. Curtin (Lincoln: University of Nebraska Press, 1970), 638; hereafter cited in the text as *WP*.

45. O'Brien considers the relationship between Valentine and Charlotte that of brother and sister, and Valentine an androgynous figure (263–64).

46. Paul Ricoeur, *Time and Narrative*, trans. Kathleen McLaughlin and David Pellauer, vol. 1 (Chicago: University of Chicago Press, 1983), chapter 1 and passim.

47. *Obscure Destinies* (1932; New York: Vintage, 1974), 59; stories in this collection are hereafter cited in the text as *OD*.

48. How Cather alludes to her own adolescent masculine-scientific phase is intriguing. In the year before the time of the story, Vickie becomes friends with a group of college boys searching for fossils. Mrs. Rosen thinks that Vickie's ambitions were affected by her admiration for the scholarly professor leading the group, but Victoria, misunderstanding, denies this: "There ain't a particle of romance in Vickie." To Mrs. Harris's satisfaction, Mrs. Rosen answers, "But there are several kinds of romance, Mrs. Templeton. She may not have your kind" (150).

49. Willa Cather to Carrie Miner Sherwood, 4 July 1932. In a letter of 27 January 1934, also to Sherwood, Cather refers to the effect of the friendship on a girl. Letters in the Willa Cather Historical Center, Red Cloud.

50. Cather told Alfred Knopf that as she wrote "Two Friends" she had in mind the paintings of Courbet (Brown, 292).

51. Willa Cather to Edith Lewis, 10 May 1936, Willa Cather Historical Center.

52. Dorothy Van Ghent, *Willa Cather*, University of Minnesota Pamphlets on American Writers, no. 36 (Minneapolis: University of Minnesota Press, 1964), 42.

53. There is a slight anachronism here, as Bernhardt did not die until 1923, and "The Old Beauty" is set in 1922. The year 1922 is frequently taken to have special significance for Cather because in her preface to *Not under Forty* (written in 1936, the same year as "The Old Beauty") she says that the world "broke in two" that year. She was undoubtedly referring to the universally accepted fact that World War I led to changes that became a great historical watershed (the background of "The Old Beauty"), but the remark is often misinterpreted as referring to her personal psychological state. In fact, Sergeant states that she was in especially good spirits at that time.

54. *Nebraska State Journal*, 25 November 1894; reprinted in *WP*, 65–66.

55. *Nebraska State Journal*, 10 January 1897; reprinted in *WP*, 472.

56. *Nebraska State Journal*, 19 January 1896; reprinted in *KA*, 166.

57. Pittsburgh *Leader*, 26 December 1897; reprinted in *WP*, 924–29.

58. *Nebraska State Journal*, 1 March 1896; reprinted in *WP*, 184.

59. This 1908 letter is quoted by Cather in her preface to Sarah Orne Jewett, *The Country of the Pointed Firs and Other Stories* (1925; Garden City, N.Y.: Anchor, 1956), n.p.

60. Richard LeGallienne, preface to Lillie Langtry, *The Days I Knew* (New York: George H. Doran, 1925), v; hereafter cited in the text.

61. At least two critics see the lively Cherry as being the true perspective of the story, and the portrait of Gabrielle a satire. See Arnold, 158–65, and Woodress, 477.

62. Hugh Kenner, *The Pound Era* (Berkeley and Los Angeles: University of California Press, 1971), 32.

63. "For Once, Then, Something," *Complete Poems of Robert Frost* (New York: Holt, Rinehart & Winston, 1949), 276.

64. See, for instance, Woodress, 473 and passim, and David Stouck, "Willa Cather's Last Four Books," in Murphy, *Critical Essays on Willa Cather*, 290–99.

Part 2

THE WRITER

Introduction

Willa Cather wished to be remembered as a writer of fiction only, not as a critic or theoretician of literature, and certainly not as a public personality. In the later years of her life, in fact, she was apt to be testy in refusing interviews and public engagements, and she saw to it that private papers and letters were not left to be published.

Before her success was assured, however, she was less chary of her privacy; she granted interviews and even gave a few speeches. After her death, memoirs and, somewhat later, biographies, appeared, gradually giving us a portrait of a woman who throughout her life was warmly engaged with friends, family, the arts, current affairs, and ideas.

I have selected items that focus on the early part of Cather's writing career, beginning with Edith Lewis's account of her first meeting with Cather in 1903. Lewis's tone throughout her reminiscence is respectful, indeed reverent, but she nevertheless has caught the dress, manner, and voice of Cather at age thirty, when she was writing the short stories that would appear in *The Troll Garden*.

The first of the four interviews reprinted here appeared in 1913; the last in 1925. In the earliest, "Willa Cather Talks of Work," Cather is more open than she would be later; further, what she says is of particular interest in regard to our view of her as a short story writer. Asked by the interviewer what she learned from reading the thousands of stories submitted to *McClure's*, Cather tries to define the elusive quality of authenticity, or sincerity, that she demands. She insists that the author's honesty can be sensed by the reader. Her novel *O Pioneers!* had just been published, and she reports that it had begun as two short stories, which she eventually joined. One might hazard that in her mind the line between the novel and the story remained an indefinite one and that she began each fiction with a situation, or human configuration, then allowed it to develop its own scope and form. That she held this organic view of story genesis is borne out by much that she said and wrote, as in the 1913 interview.

The next two interviews, both from 1921, following the publication of *My Ántonia*, give interesting pictures of Cather's strong, definite manner and opinions. The second of the two speaks of her ambivalent attachment to the West of her childhood.

The final interview, "Glimpses of Interesting Americans," describes the Washington Square area of New York City, where for a number of years Cather and Edith Lewis shared an apartment. Cather here speaks movingly of her need to hear American speech. She could never be an expatriate writer, however much she loved England and France.

In 1925 Cather gave one of her rare public speeches, the occasion being a literary festival at Bowdoin College. The program included readings and talks by Robert Frost, Edna St. Vincent Millay, John Dos Passos, Irving Babbitt, and Carl Sandburg. Cather's speech, on the technique of writing, has not survived, but the newspaper account reprinted here at least gives a notion of her topics. Of greatest interest is the distinction she makes between the "spiritual" and the "crude" plot, and her disparagement of plot as such.

The final item reprinted here is her essay "The Novel Démeublé," which appeared in the *New Republic* in 1922. Appropriately brief, it is Cather's most important statement of her aesthetic beliefs and contains a number of intriguing comments, among them her much-repeated observation concerning "the inexplicable presence of the thing not named." This small essay is as close to a statement of creed as Cather would come. Fastidious selectivity, reticence, control—these principles governed both her life and her art.

Willa Cather Living

Edith Lewis

How deeply one takes impressions when one is young! In that first meeting I think I felt, without at all formulating it, all that was really essential in what I afterward came to know of Willa Cather. When the maid showed me into the parlour, Willa Cather and Sarah Harris [publisher of the Lincoln *Courier*] were having a spirited discussion about something,—I have no idea what—and after I was introduced, they paid no attention to me, but continued their conversation. Willa Cather, a rather slim figure, in a grey and white striped cotton dress, was sitting very upright in a straight-backed chair. She had curling chestnut-brown hair, done high on her head, a fair skin; but the feature one noticed particularly was her eyes. They were dark blue eyes, with dark lashes; and I know no way of describing them, except to say that they were the eyes of genius. I have never met any very gifted person who did not have extraordinary eyes. Many people's eyes, I have noticed, are half opaque; they conceal, as much as they express, their owner's personality, and thought, feeling, struggle through them like light through a clouded sky. But Willa Cather's eyes were like a direct communication of her spirit. The whole of herself was in her look, in that transparently clear, level, unshrinking gaze that seemed to know everything there was to be known about both herself and you.

I had been silent, a fascinated spectator, while Willa Cather and Sarah Harris carried on their duel of words; but when I got up to go, Willa Cather accompanied me to the door, and there she stood and talked with me for fifteen or twenty minutes, giving me her whole attention. She talked to me as if we were fellow-students, both pursuing the same vocation. (Sarah Harris had published one or two of my college themes in the *Courier;* she loved to encourage young people, and besides, she had to fill up her space every week, and had almost no money to pay for contributions; but her Burlington brothers could always get free transportation for her, and she would reward me with passes to Omaha and to Colorado.)

Willa Cather asked me how many hours a day I worked, and what I found the best time of the day for writing; what I liked best to write about. I do not think it was tact, or that she was trying to put me at ease. She had always a warm, eager, spontaneous interest in people. It was impossible for her to make a perfunctory approach to anyone; she wanted at once to get beneath the surface, to find out what they were really like.

I met her once or twice again before she went on to Pittsburgh. She seemed struck by the fact that I was planning to go that Fall to New York to try and get myself a job there—any kind of job. She asked me to stop over in Pittsburgh on my way, and spend a night at the house of Judge McClung, where she was then living.

If I have described this slight encounter at more length than it seems to deserve, it is because it was one of those unimportant incidents that later, when seen from a long perspective, become to one very important. If I had not met Willa Cather at this time, the chances are that I would never have met her, and our long friendship and association, which lasted until her death, would never have happened.

I went to New York that Fall, and rented what was called a "studio" on the south side of Washington Square, and there Willa Cather visited me for a week the following summer. She was working then, when she had any time off from teaching, on the short stories that afterward appeared in her first prose volume, *The Troll Garden*. I had a small job with the Century Publishing Co., and I remember asking her to let me take one of these stories to show an officer of the company whom I knew; but he regretfully though kindly declined it, saying that for the *Century Magazine* they preferred stories "about equally combining humour and pathos."

The following summer (1905) Willa Cather came again to New York, and stayed with me for a longer time. Two of her stories had been published in *McClure's Magazine* in the early months of 1905, and it was probably before her New York visit that S. S. McClure, with his usual enterprise, made a flying trip to Pittsburgh to see her, and arranged to bring out a collection of her stories in book form. It never took Mr. McClure any time at all to make up his mind about people. *The Troll Garden* was published in the Fall of 1905; and in 1906 Willa Cather gave up her teaching job in Pittsburgh, and accepted his offer of a staff position on *McClure's Magazine*.

It was not without some trepidation that she made this change. She was naturally a very fearless person, fearless in matters of thought, of social convention; people never intimidated her; and she was extremely self-possessed in the presence of physical danger. But ever since her college days, when the crops failed in Nebraska, and her family were struggling along on very little money; when in order to complete her college course she began writing copy at a dollar a column for the *Nebraska State Journal*—she had known how hard and humiliating poverty can be. Her first years in Pittsburgh were years of constant worry about money; and she was not very confident of ever being able to make her living successfully. It was dazzling to think of becoming an editor on *McClure's Magazine* at a much higher salary than she was then earning; but how long would it last? Her teaching job was safe and sure, and she had her summer vacations to write in.

She took a studio for the first few months at 60 South Washington Square, the house in which I was then living. In 1906, Washington Square was one of the most charming places in New York. On the north side the long row of houses of rose-red brick, residences of aristocratic old New York families, gave it an aura of gentility and dignity. On the south side, writers and artists lived. But it was a very sedate Bohemia; most of the artists were poor and hardworking. In *Coming, Aphrodite!*, the opening story in *Youth and the Bright Medusa*, Willa Cather has recalled not only the physical aspects of the old studio building at Number 60 and its surrounding neighborhood, but even more, the youthful, lighthearted, and rather poetic mood of those days before the automobile, the radio, the moving picture—and before two wars. As I look back, it seems to me that young people were younger then—more ingenuous, less initiated. Life seemed more unknown to them—and its possibilities more boundless.

Willa Cather was then about thirty. I think it is her talk that I remember best. It was not that she talked a great deal. She was never a monologist; and one often felt that she enjoyed silence more than conversation. But whatever she said had an evocative quality—a quality of creating much more than her words actually stated, of summoning up images, suggestions, overtones and undertones of feeling that opened long vistas to one's imagination. Her talk was sometimes more brilliant than her writing; for it had the freer quality of improvisation. Thought and language seemed simultaneous with her, as if one did not have to be translated into the other; she rarely had to search or struggle for a word or phrase.

And her voice always took on the colour of what she was saying. It could be harsh, hard, when she felt scornful of something. But when anything moved her deeply, it often had a low, muted, very musical quality. It had many shades and variations. One could usually tell by the tone of her voice whether she liked, admired the person she was talking to.

I remember her then as brimming over with vitality, with eagerness for life. The city itself, so open to the sea and freedom, the people she met on McClure's, the work she was doing, all stimulated and excited her. She welcomed every new experience with vivid enjoyment. And yet, even then, with all her natural ardour and high spirits, I think that, unperceived by most of the people who knew her, there was in her also a deep strain of melancholy. It did not often emerge. Perhaps it even gave intensity to her delight in things—this sense that human destiny was ultimately, and necessarily, tragic.

Soon after Willa Cather joined the McClure staff, which was then being completely reorganized, owing to the exodus of John Phillips, Miss Tarbell, and their associates, an opening for an editorial proof-reader came about; and Willa Cather urged me to try for it. Will Irwin was then managing editor of McClure's. I applied to him, and was given the job. During the year or more that Willa Cather was working in Boston on the Christian Science articles—her first McClure assignment—I was sent often to Boston to read proofs with her. This was the beginning of our working together. From the time that she wrote *The Song of the Lark*, we read together the copy and proofs of all her books. It was one of our greatest pleasures.

I stayed on at McClure's until two years after Willa Cather left the magazine, working with Cameron Mackenzie as assistant managing editor: so that in those eight years I came to know well the people and conditions on McClure's, and in what way they affected Willa Cather. About 1909 we took an apartment together on Washington Place, and here she wrote her first novel, *Alexander's Bridge*.

I have tried, in this brief introduction, to trace the outline of how our friendship began.

Willa Cather Talks of Work

Miss Willa Sibert Cather, whose new novel, *O Pioneers!* has just placed her in the foremost rank of American novelists, began to do newspaper work on the *Nebraska State Journal* while she was still an undergraduate in the University at Lincoln. From Lincoln Miss Cather came East as far as Pittsburgh, to go on the regular staff of the *Daily Leader.*

Leaving the newspaper life, while still very young, Miss Cather then accepted a position to teach, first Latin and afterward English, in the Pittsburgh High School. It was during this time that she wrote the verse and short stories which secured her the post of associate editor of *McClure's Magazine* and took her finally to New York.

Miss Cather's new novel, *O Pioneers!* is of special interest to Philadelphians—this magnificently grave and simple and poetic picture of early days on the uplands of Nebraska—if only for the strong influence of Whitman which the writing shows. There is the wise, clean-earthed philosophy of Whitman in the selection of the book's theme, too, and Miss Cather quotes her title direct from our superb white-bearded old lover of the world.

Though Miss Cather no longer spends all her time in the McClure Publications offices, on Fourth Avenue (she was managing editor of *McClure's Magazine* for four years), she is still connected with that publishing house; and I was eager to have her opinion of modern short-story writing in the United States.

"My own favorite American writers?" said Miss Cather. "Well, I've never changed in that respect much since I was a girl at school. There were great ones I liked best then and still like—Mark Twain, Henry James and Sarah Orne Jewett."

"You must have read a lot of work by new people while you were editor of *McClure's?*" I suggested.

This article originally appeared in the 10 August 1913 *Philadelphia Record* and is reprinted from *Willa Cather in Person: Interviews, Speeches, and Letters,* selected and edited by L. Brent Bohlke (Lincoln: University of Nebraska Press, 1986), 7–11. © 1986 by the University of Nebraska Press. Reprinted by permission of the University of Nebraska Press.

"Yes," smiled Miss Cather, "I suppose I read a good many thousand stories, some good and some bad."

"And what seemed to you to be the trouble with most of the mediocre ones?"

"Simply this," replied Miss Cather unhesitatingly, "that the writer had not felt them strongly enough before he wrote them. Like everything else in the world, this is a question of—how far. No one person knows much more about writing than another. I expect that when people think they know anything about it, then their case is hopeless. But in my course of reading thousands of stories, I was strengthened in the conclusion that I had come to before; that nothing was really worth while that did not cut pretty deep, and that the main thing always was to be honest.

"So many of the stories that come into magazines are a combination of the genuine and the fake. A writer has really a story to tell, and he has evidently tried to make it fit the outline of some story that he admires, or that he believes has been successful. You can not always tell just where a writer stops being himself and begins to attitudinize in a story, but when you finish it, you have a feeling that he has been trying to fool himself. I think a writer ought to get into his copy as he really is, in his everyday clothes. His readers are thrown with him in a personal relation, just as if they were traveling with him; and if he is not sincere, there is no possibility of any sort of comradeship.

"I think many story writers try to multiply their ideas instead of trying to simplify them; that is, they often try to make a story out of every idea they have, to get returns on every situation that suggests itself. And, as a result, their work is entertaining, journalistic and thin. Whether it is a pianist, or a singer, or a writer, art ought to simplify—that seems to me to be the whole process. Millet did hundreds of sketches of peasants sowing grain, some of then very complicated, but when he came to paint 'The Sower,' the composition is so simple that it seems inevitable. It was probably the hundred sketches that went before that made the picture what it finally became—a process of simplifying all the time—of sacrificing many things that were in themselves interesting and pleasing, and all the time getting closer to the one thing—It.

"Of course I am talking now about the kind of writing that interests me most—I take it that is what you want me to do. There is *The Three Guardsmen* kind, which is, perhaps, quite as fine in its way, where the whole zest of the thing is the rapid multiplication of fancies and devices. That kind of writing, at its best, is like fencing and dancing, the games that live forever. But the other kind, the kind that I am talking about, is pretty well summed up in a letter of Miss Sarah Orne Jewett's, that I found among some of her papers in South Berwick after her death:

"'Ah, it is things like that, which haunt the mind for years, and at last write themselves down, that belong, whether little or great, to literature.'

"It is that kind of honesty, that earnest endeavor to tell truly the thing that haunts the mind, that I love in Miss Jewett's own work. Reading her books from the beginning one finds that often she tried a character or a theme over and over, first in one story and then in another, before she at last realized it completely on the page. That wonderful story, 'Martha's Lady,' for instance, was hinted at and felt for in several of her earlier stories. And so was the old woman in 'The Queen's Twin.'

"I dedicated my novel *O Pioneers!* to Miss Jewett because I had talked over some of the characters in it with her one day at Manchester, and in this book I tried to tell the story of the people as truthfully and simply as if I were telling it to her by word of mouth."

"How did you come to write about that flat part of the prairie west, Miss Cather, which not many people find interesting?"

"I happen to be interested in the Scandinavian and Bohemian pioneers of Nebraska," said the young novelist, "because I lived among them when I was a child. When I was eight years old, my father moved from the Shenandoah Valley in Virginia to that Western country. My grandfather and grandmother had moved to Nebraska eight years before we left Virginia; they were among the real pioneers.

"But it was still wild enough and bleak enough when we got there. My grandfather's homestead was about eighteen miles from Red Cloud—a little town on the Burlington, named after the old Indian chief who used to come hunting in that country, and who buried his daughter on the top of one of the river bluffs south of the town. Her grave had been looted for her rich furs and beadwork long before my family went West, but we children used to find arrowheads there and some of the bones of her pony that had been strangled above her grave."

"What was the country like when you got there?"

"I shall never forget my introduction to it. We drove out from Red Cloud to my grandfather's homestead one day in April. I was sitting on the hay in the bottom of a Studebaker wagon, holding on to the wide of the wagon box to steady myself—the roads were mostly faint trails over the bunch grass in those days. The land was open range and there was almost no fencing. As we drove further and further out into the country, I felt a good deal as if we had come to the end of everything—it was a kind of erasure of personality.

"I would not know how much a child's life is bound up in the woods and hills and meadows around it, if I had not been jerked away from all these and thrown out into a country as bare as a piece of sheet iron. I had heard my father say you had to show grit in a new country, and I would have got on pretty well during that ride if it had not been for the larks. Every now and then one flew up and sang a few splendid notes and dropped down into the grass again. That reminded me of something—I don't know what, but my one purpose in life just then was not to cry, and every time they did it, I thought I should go under.

"For the first week or two on the homestead I had that kind of contraction of the stomach which comes from homesickness. I didn't like canned things anyhow, and I made an agreement with myself that I would not eat much until I got back to Virginia and could get some fresh mutton. I think the first thing that interested me after I got to the homestead was a heavy hickory cane with a steel tip which my grandmother always carried with her when she went to the garden to kill rattlesnakes. She had killed a good many snakes with it, and that seemed to argue that life might not be so flat as it looked there.

"We had very few American neighbors—they were mostly Swedes and Danes, Norwegians and Bohemians. I liked them from the first and they made up for what I missed in the country. I particularly liked the old women, they understood my homesickness and were kind to me. I had met 'traveled' people in Virginia and in Washington, but these old women on the farms were the first people who ever gave me the real feeling of an older world across the sea. Even when they spoke very little English, the old women somehow managed to tell me a great many stories about the old country. They talk more freely to a child than to grown people, and I always felt as if every word they said to me counted for twenty.

"I have never found any intellectual excitement any more intense than I used to feel when I spent a morning with one of those old women at her baking or butter making. I used to ride home in the most unreasonable state of excitement; I always felt as if they told me so much more than they said—as if I had actually got inside another person's skin. If one begins that early, it is the story of the maneating tiger over again—no other adventure ever carries one quite so far."

"Some of your early short stories were about these people, were they not?"

"Yes, but most of them were poor. It is always hard to write about the things that are near to your heart, from a kind of instinct of self-protection you distort them and disguise them. Those stories were so poor that they discouraged me. I decided that I wouldn't write any more about the country and people for which I had such personal feeling.

"Then I had the good fortune to meet Sarah Orne Jewett, who had read all of my early stories and had very clear and definite opinions about them and about where my work fell short. She said, 'Write it as it is, don't try to make it like this or that. You can't do it in anybody else's way—you will have to make a way of your own. If the way happens to be new, don't let that frighten you. Don't try to write the kind of short story that this or that magazine wants—write the truth, and let them take it or leave it.'

"I was not at all sure, however, that my feeling about the Western country and my Scandinavian friends was the truth—I thought perhaps that going among them so young I had a romantic personal feeling about them. I thought that Americans in general must see only the humorous side of the Scandinavian—the side often presented in vaudeville dialect sketches—because nobody had ever tried to write about the Swedish settlers seriously.

"What has pleased me most in the cordial reception the West has given this new book of mine, is that the reviewers in all those Western States say the thing seems to them true to the country and the people. That is a great satisfaction. The reviews have concerned themselves a good deal more with the subject matter of the story than with my way of telling it, and I am glad of that. I care a lot more about the country and the people than I care about my own way of writing or anybody else's way of writing."

Willa Cather

Eleanor Hinman

"The old-fashioned farmer's wife is nearer to the type of the true artist and the prima donna than is the culture enthusiast," declared Miss Willa Cather, author of *The Song of the Lark*, *O Pioneers!*, *My Ántonia*, *Youth and the Bright Medusa*, who has earned the title of one of the foremost American novelists by her stories of prima donnas and pioneers. She was emphasizing that the two are not so far apart in type as most people seem to imagine.

Miss Cather had elected to take her interview out-of-doors in the autumnal sunshine, walking. The fact is characteristic. She is an outdoor person, not far different in type from the pioneers and prima donnas whom she exalts.

She walks with the gait of one who has been used to the saddle. Her complexion is firm with an outdoor wholesomeness. The red in her cheeks is the red that comes from the bite of the wind. Her voice is deep, rich, and full of color; she speaks with her whole body, like a singer.

"Downright" is the word that comes most often to the mind in thinking of her. Whatever she does is done with every fibre. There is no pretense in her, and no conventionality. In conversation she is more stimulating than captivating. She has ideas and is not afraid to express them. Her mind scintillates and sends rays of light down many avenues of thought.

When the interviewer was admitted to her, she was pasting press clippings on a huge sheet of brown wrapping paper, as whole-heartedly as though it were the most important action of her life.

"This way you get them all together," she explained, "and you can see who it is that really likes you, who that really hates you, and who that actually hates you but pretends to like you. I don't mind the ones that hate me; I don't doubt they have good reasons; but I despise the ones that pretend."

When she had finished, she went to her room and almost immediately came out of it again, putting on her hat and coat as she came

From the *Lincoln Sunday Star*, 6 November 1921. Reprinted by permission.

down the stairs, and going out without a glance at the mirror. She dresses well, yet she is clearly one of the women to whom the chief requirement of clothes is that they should be clean and comfortable. Although she is very fond of walking, it is evidently strictly subordinate in her mind to conversation. The stroll was perpetually slowing down to a crawl and stopping short at some point which required emphasis. She has a characteristic gesture to bring out a cardinal point; it commences as though it would be a hearty clap upon the shoulder of the person whom she is addressing, but it checks itself and ends without even a touch.

I had intended to interview her on how she gathers the material for her writings; but walking leads to discursiveness and it would be hard to assemble the whole interview under any more definite topic than that bugbear of authors, "an author's views on art." But the longer Miss Cather talks, the more one is filled with the conviction that life is a fascinating business and one's own experience more fascinating than one had ever suspected it of being. Some persons have this gift of infusing their own abundant vitality into the speaker, as Roosevelt is said to have done.

"I don't gather the material for my stories," declared Miss Cather. "All my stories have been written with material that was gathered— no, God save us! not gathered but absorbed—before I was fifteen years old. Other authors tell me it is the same way with them. Sarah Orne Jewett insisted to me that she has used nothing in all her short stories which she did not remember before she was eight years old.

"People will tell you that I come west to get ideas for a new novel, or material for a new novel, as though a novel could be conceived by running around with a pencil and [paper] and jotting down phrases and suggestions. I don't even come west for local color.

"I could not say, however, that I don't come west for Inspiration. I do get freshened up by coming out here. I like to go back to my home town, Red Cloud, and get out among the folk who like me for myself, who don't know and don't care a thing about my books, and who treat me just as they did before I published any of them. It makes me feel just like a kid!" cried Willa Cather, writer of finely polished prose.

"The ideas for all my novels have come from things that happened around Red Cloud when I was a child. I was all over the country then, on foot, on horseback and in our farm wagons. My nose went poking into nearly everything. It happened that my mind was constructed for the particular purpose of absorbing impressions and retaining them. I always intended to write, and there were certain persons I studied. I seldom had much idea of the plot or the other characters, but I used my eyes and my ears."

Miss Cather described in detail the way in which the book *My Ántonia* took form in her mind. This is the most recent of her novels; its scene is laid in Nebraska, and it is evidently a favorite of hers.

"One of the people who interested me most as a child was the Bohemian hired girl of one of our neighbors, who was so good to me. She was one of the truest artists I ever knew in the keenness and sensitiveness of her enjoyment, in her love of people and in her willingness to take pains. I did not realize all this as a child, but Annie fascinated me, and I always had it in mind to write a story about her.

"But from what point of view should I write it up? I might give her a lover and write from his standpoint. However, I thought my Ántonia deserved something better than the *Saturday Evening Post* sort of stuff in her book. Finally I concluded that I would write from the point of a detached observer, because that was what I had always been.

"Then, I noticed that much of what I knew about Annie came from the talks I had with young men. She had a fascination for them, and they used to be with her whenever they could. They had to manage it on the sly, because she was only a hired girl. But they respected and admired her, and she meant a good deal to some of them. So I decided to make my observer a young man.

"There was the material in that book for a lurid melodrama. But I decided that in writing it I would dwell very lightly upon those things that a novelist would ordinarily emphasize and make up my story of the little, every-day happenings and occurrences that form the greatest part of everyone's life and happiness.

"After all, it is the little things that really matter most, the unfinished things, the things that never quite come to birth. Sometimes a man's wedding day is the happiest day in his life; but usually he likes most of all to look back upon some quite simple, quite uneventful day when nothing in particular happened but all the world seemed touched with gold. Sometimes it is a man's wife who sums up to him his ideal of all a woman can be; but how often it is some girl whom he scarcely knows, whose beauty and kindliness have caught at his imagination without cloying it!"

It was many years after the conception of the story that it was written. This story of Nebraska was finally brought to birth in the White

Mountains. And Miss Cather's latest novel, which will be published next fall, and which alone of all her prairie stories deals with the Nebraska of the present, was written largely on the Mediterranean coast in southern France, where its author has been during the past spring and summer.

It is often related that Miss Cather draws the greater part of her characters from the life, that they are actually portraits of individual people. This statement she absolutely denies.

"I have never drawn but one portrait of an actual person. That was the mother of the neighbor family, in *My Ántonia*. She was the mother of my childhood chums in Red Cloud. I used her so for this reason: While I was getting under way with the book in the White Mountains, I received the word of her death. One clings to one's friends so—I don't know why it was—but the resolve came over me that I would put her into that book as nearly drawn from the life as I could do it. I had not seen her for years.

"I have always been so glad that I did so, because her daughters were so deeply touched. When the book was published it recalled to them little traits of hers that they had not remembered of themselves— as, for example, that when she was vexed she used to dig her heels into the floor as she walked and go clump! clump! clump! across the floor. They cannot speak of the book without weeping.

"All my other characters are drawn from life, but they are all composites of three or four persons. I do not quite understand it, but certain persons seem to coalesce naturally when one is working up a story. I believe most authors shrink from actual portrait painting. It seems so cold-blooded, so heartless, so indecent almost, to present an actual person in that intimate fashion, stripping his very soul."

Although Miss Cather's greatest novels all deal with Nebraska, and although it has been her work which has first put Nebraska upon the literary map, this seems to have been more a matter of necessity with her than of choice. For when she was asked to give her reflections about Nebraska as a storehouse of literary or artistic material, her answer was not altogether conciliatory.

"Of course Nebraska is a storehouse of literary material. Everywhere is a storehouse of literary material. If a true artist was born in a pigpen and raised in a sty, he would still find plenty of inspiration for his work. The only need is the eye to see.

"Generally speaking, the older and more established the civilization, the better a subject it is for art. In an old community there has been time for associations to gather and for interesting types to develop. People do not feel that they all must be exactly alike.

"At present in the west there seems to be an idea that we all must be like somebody else, as much as if we had all been cast in the same mold. We wear exactly similar clothes, drive the same make of car, live in the same part of town, in the same style of house. It's deadly! Not long ago one of my dear friends said to me that she was about to move.

" 'Oh,' I cried, 'how can you leave this beautiful old house!'

" 'Well,' she said, 'I don't really want to go, but all our friends have moved to the other end of town, and we have lived in this house for forty years.'

"What better reason can you want for staying in a house than that you have lived there for forty years?

"New things are always ugly. New clothes are always ugly. A prima donna will never wear a new gown upon the stage. She wears it first around her apartment until is shapes itself to her figure; or if she hasn't time to do that, she hires an understudy to wear it. A house can never be beautiful until it has been lived in for a long time. An old house built and furnished in miserable taste is more beautiful than a new house built and furnished in correct taste. The beauty lies in the associations that cluster around it, the way in which the house has fitted itself to the people.

"This rage for newness and conventionality is one of the things which I deplore in the present-day Nebraska. The second is the prevalence of a superficial culture. These women who run about from one culture club to another studying Italian art out of a textbook and an encyclopedia and believing that they are learning something about it by memorizing a string of facts, are fatal to the spirit of art. The nigger boy who plays by ear on his fiddle airs from *Traviata* without knowing what he is playing, or why he likes it, has more real understanding of Italian art than these esthetic creatures with a head and a larynx, and no organs that they get any use of, who reel you off the life of Leonardo da Vinci.

"Art is a matter of enjoyment through the five senses. Unless you can see the beauty all around you everywhere, and enjoy it, you can never comprehend art. Take the cottonwood, for example, the most beautiful tree on the plains. The people of Paris go crazy about them. They have planted long boulevards with them. They hold one of their fetes when the cotton begins to fly; they call it 'summer snow.' But people of Red Cloud and Hastings chop them down.

"Take our Nebraska wild flowers. There is no place in the world that has more beautiful ones. But they have no common names. In England, in any European country, they would all have beautiful names like eglantine, primrose, and celandine. As a child I gave them all names of my own. I used to gather great armfuls of them and sit and cry over them. They were so lovely, and no one seemed to care for them at all! There is one book that I would rather have produced than all my novels. That is the Clemens botany dealing with the wild flowers of the west.

"But why am I taking so many examples from one sense? Esthetic appreciation begins with the enjoyment of the morning bath. It should include all the activities of life. There is real art in cooking a roast just right, so that it is brown and dripping and odorous and 'saignant.'

"The farmer's wife who raises a large family and cooks for them and makes their clothes and keeps house and on the side runs a truck garden and a chicken farm and a canning establishment, and thoroughly enjoys doing it all, and doing it well, contributes more to art than all the culture clubs. Often you find such a woman with all the appreciation of the beautiful bodies of her children, of the order and harmony of her kitchen, of the real creative joy of all her activities, which marks the great artist.

"Most of the women artists I have known—the prima donnas, novelists, poets, sculptors—have been women of this same type. The very best cooks I have ever known have been prima donnas. When I visited them the way to their hearts was the same as to the hearts of the pioneer rancher's wife in my childhood—I must eat a great deal, and enjoy it.

"Many people seem to think that art is a luxury to be imported and tacked on to life. Art springs out of the very stuff that life is made of. Most of our young authors start to write a story and make a few observations from nature to add local color. The results are invariably false and hollow. Art must spring out of the fullness and the richness of life."

This glorification of the old-fashioned housewife came very naturally from Willa Cather, chronicler of women with careers. What does Miss Cather think of the present movement of women into business and the arts?

"It cannot help but be good," was her reply. "It at least keeps the woman interested in something real.

"As for the choice between a woman's home and her career, is there any reason why she cannot have both? In France the business is regarded as a family affair. It is taken for granted that Madame will be the business partner of her husband; his bookkeeper, cashier or whatever she fits best. Yet the French women are famous housekeepers and their children do not suffer for lack of care.

"The situation is similar if the woman's business is art. Her family life will be a help rather than a hindrance to her; and if she has a quarter of the vitality of her prototype on the farm she will be able to fulfill the claims of both."

Miss Cather, however, deplores heartily the drift of the present generation away from the land.

"All the farmer's sons and daughters seem to want to get into the professions where they think they may find a soft place. 'I'm sure not going to work the way the old man did,' seems to be the slogan of today. Soon only the Swedes and Germans will be left to uphold the prosperity of the country."

She contrasts the university of the present with that in the lean days of the nineties, "when," as she says, "the ghosts walked in this country." She came to Lincoln, a child barely in her teens, with her own way to make absolutely. She lived on thirty dollars a month, worked until 1 or 2 o'clock every night, ate no breakfast in the morning by way of saving time and money, never really had enough to eat, and carried full college work. "And many of the girls I was with were much worse off than I." Yet the large majority of the famous alumni of the university date from precisely this period of hard work and little cash.

In making her way into the literary world she never had, she declares, half the hardships that she endured in this battle for an education. Her first book of short stories, to be sure, was a bitter disappointment. Few people bought it, and her Nebraska friends could find no words bad enough for it. "They wanted me to write propaganda for the commercial club," she explained.

"An author is seldom sensitive except about his first volume. Any criticism of that hurts. Not criticism of its style—that only spurs one on to improve it. But the root-and-branch kind of attack is hard to forget. Nearly all very young authors write sad stories and very many of them write their first stories in revolt against everything. Humor, kindliness, tolerance come later."

Some of the stories from this unsuccessful volume, *The Troll Garden,* were reprinted in *Youth and the Bright Medusa,* the recent volume which has had a wide success.

Miss Cather spent Monday, Tuesday, and Wednesday with Mrs. Max Westerman, going from here to Omaha to deliver a lecture before the fine arts club.

How Willa Cather Found Herself

Eva Mahoney

Miss Cather tells about those years of tireless effort as follows:

"When I left the University of Nebraska after graduating and went to New York City, I wanted to write after the best style of Henry James—the foremost mind that ever applied itself to literature in America. I was dazzled. I was trying to work in a sophisticated medium and write about highly developed people whom I knew only superficially.

"It was during the six years when I was editor of *McClure's* magazine that I came to have a definite idea about writing. In reading manuscripts submitted to me, I found that 95 percent of them were written for the sake of the writer—never for the sake of the material. The writer wanted to express his clever ideas, his wit, his observations. Almost never did I find a manuscript that was written because a writer loved his subject so much he had to write about it.

"Usually," she added, "when I did get such a manuscript it was so crude it was ineffective. Then I realized that one must have two things—strong enough to mate together without either killing the other—else one had better change his job. I learned that a man must have a technique and a birthright to write—I do not know how else to express it. He must know his subject with an understanding that passes understanding—like the babe knows its own mother's breast."

It was through this critical analysis of story writing that Miss Cather finally found herself. "I had been trying to sing a song that did not lie in my voice," Miss Cather declared.

"There I was on the Atlantic coast among dear and helpful friends and surrounded by the great masters and teachers with all their tradition of learning and culture, and yet I was always being pulled back into Nebraska," she continued. "Whenever I crossed the Missouri river coming into Nebraska the very smell of the soil tore me to pieces. I could not decide which was the real and which the fake 'me.' I almost decided to settle down on a quarter section of land and let my writing go. My deepest affection was not for the other people and the other

From the Omaha *World-Herald*, 27 November 1921. Reprinted by permission.

places I had been writing about. I loved the country where I had been a kid, where they still called me 'Willie' Cather.

"I knew every farm, every tree, every field in the region around my home, and they all called out to me," she added earnestly. "My deepest feelings were rooted in this country because one's strongest emotions and one's most vivid mental pictures are acquired before one is 15. I had searched for books telling about the beauty of the country I loved, its romance, and heroism and strength and courage of its people that had been plowed into the very furrows of its soil, and I did not find them. And so I wrote *O Pioneers!*."

And in the writing of this book and the other books that followed, Willa Cather saw all those early years had been in preparation for her rightful task. Out of her experience with complex people and complex things had come a great work of literature about simple people and simple things.

This, too, Sarah Orne Jewett had epitomized for Miss Cather when she said to her: "You have to know the world so well before you know the parish," and so after coming to know the world, Miss Cather went back home and wrote about the parish.

Another literary friend, Dorothy Canfield Fisher, has recently written in the *Yale Review* in unreserved praise of Miss Cather's work. Strangely enough Miss Cather and Mrs. Fisher were schoolmates at the University of Nebraska, and now both are writers of national distinction. Mrs. Fisher wrote as follows:

"There is no writer living in whose excellence Americans feel a warmer, prouder pleasure than we all feel in the success of Willa Cather. I do not mean by success the wide recognition given her, although that is delightful to see. I mean what must give much more satisfaction to Miss Cather, herself, her real inner success, her real excellence, her firm, steady upward growth and expansion into tranquil and assured power. It is as heartening and inspiring a spectacle as the rich, healthful growth and flowering into splendor of a plant in our gardens, for she is a plant of our own American garden to her last fiber.

"Here is an American to whom European culture (and she has always had plenty of that) is but food to be absorbed and transformed into a new product, quite different, unique, inimitable, with a harmonious perfection of its own. I cannot imagine any exercise which would be of more use to a young writer than to take the last story in her new volume, *Youth and the Bright Medusa* (what an inspired title!), and compare it line by line with the original version which was published in the

January number of *Scribner's* in 1903. The whole story of Miss Cather's development is there, and an uninformed writer would learn more by pondering on the changes made by Miss Cather in her own story after eighteen years of growth and work than by listening to many lectures from the professors of literature.

"So often writers, even very clever ones, spoil their earlier work when they try to alter it, have not the firm mastery of their craft to know how to smooth out the crudeness without rooting out the life, are so startled by the changes in their own taste that they do not know where to begin. Miss Cather, conscious, firm-willed artist that she is, has known just where to lay her finger on the false passages and how to lift them without destroying the life of the story."

In her New York home, Miss Cather works but three hours a day—hours of perfect joy and happiness, she describes them. She finds that at the end of two or three hours she has exhausted her best efforts. She spends the remainder of the day with her friends, or taking a walk in Central park, or listening to good music or busying herself with housework and forgets about her work. She believes that a writer should keep in as good physical condition as a singer, and so she regulates her life on a simple, normal schedule. She writes easily and seldom tears a paragraph or a page to pieces. She sometimes revises, but she does not fuss over her writing. "I let life flow along the pages," says this consummate artist.

Miss Cather has completed a new book, *One of Ours*. It is now in proof form. She worked three years on this book, and she considers it her best effort.

"The hero is just a red-headed prairie boy," said Miss Cather. "I always felt it was presumptuous and silly for a woman to write about a male character, but by a chain of circumstances I came to know that boy better than I know myself. I have cut out all descriptive work in this book—the thing I do best. I have cut out all picture making because that boy does not see pictures. It was hard to cease to do the thing that I do best, but we all have to pay the price for everything we accomplish, and because I was willing to pay so much to write about this boy, I felt that I had a right to do so."

Lucky prairie boy! To have Willa Cather to write about him.

Glimpses of Interesting Americans: Willa Sibert Cather

Walter Tittle

Penetrating westward from Washington Square one crosses an area devoted, in recent years, to an industry that may be described by the name that this locality bore when it was a settlement separate from New York. Greenwich Village is now a business, carried on in the spot where the little town of that name once stood. One does not need to be old to remember when its streets were quiet, at least when evening fell; but now it is the haunt of Bohemianism, Incorporated, where from humble beginnings that were more sincere have risen myriad dance-halls, taxi-stands, tea-shops, theaters, and cabarets with *couvert* charges and like ostentations that promise soon to rival Broadway. Persevere still farther west, and one is rewarded. This modern commerce has not yet obliterated all of the former charm. The crooked streets again resume their quiet, and an Old World touch is contributed by occasional lingering architectural fragments of Georgian flavor. In this pleasant back-water I found the dwelling of Willa Sibert Cather.

In response to my ring came Miss Cather herself, with a friendly smile, and a cordial greeting that seemed particularly hospitable because of its unmistakable flavor of my own Middle West. Her fine blue eyes revealed in their possessor the precious gift of humor, and contrasted pleasantly in their color with her dark lashes and strongly marked brows. Her straight, almost black, glistening hair, growing very low on her forehead, was caught back with effective simplicity from a parting just off the middle, and the harmony of it with her slightly olive skin and a colorful shawl or scarf made a picture that cried for a full palette rather than black and white.

No sooner were we settled, with pose and lighting selected, than tea appeared, bringing with it vivid memories of the importance of this unfailing comfort and promoter of sociability in England. I remarked on the great degree to which social life in that country hinges on this daily function, and discovered that for her the association bore recol-

Excerpted from *Century Magazine,* July 1925.

lections as pleasant as my own. A further pursuit of the subject revealed friends and acquaintances in common, yielding material for a considerable comparison of notes and much entertaining reminiscence. Included in this was an interesting word-portrait of Swinburne, whom she had met by chance at the British Museum with Sir Sidney Colvin. She pictured him as being far removed in reality from Watts's rather sugary portrait of him—a dwarf with a large head and abnormally tiny hands and feet. His stringy blond hair stayed horribly young where he was old, giving an uncanny effect that one could see repeated in the mummy room of the museum where they met. His manner betrayed a self-conscious timidity that seemed to indicate a pitiful sensitiveness to his physical deficiencies.

"Aren't you tempted to desert your native land and live abroad? It is easy for writers to go where they choose, their necessary impedimenta being small."

"No, I cannot do my work abroad. I hate to leave France or England when I am there, but I cannot produce any kind of work away from the American idiom. It touches springs of memory, awaking past experience and knowledge necessary to my work. I write only of the Mid-Western American life that I know thoroughly, and I must be here, where the stream of that life flowing over me touches springs that release early-caught and assimilated impressions. I cannot create my kind of thing without American speech around me and incidents that cause memories to rise from the subconscious. This is probably not true of all writers, but it is of me. I stayed for a time at Ville d'Avray, and loved the life there so much that I could hardly tear myself away; but I was so busy drinking in the beauty of the place that I could not work. Those wonderful French skies! They fascinated me. They are so different from the usual hard, bright skies of New York. I went from there to Paris, hoping to achieve a working state of mind, but again it proved impossible. The Seine absorbed my thoughts. I could look at it for hours as it reflected every mood of the ever-changing skies, and the colorful life surging around me was utterly distracting as well.

"The American language works on my mind like light on a photographic plate, or on a pack of them, creeping in at the edges. In Paris, whatever it is that makes one work got used up from day to day. New York has no such effect upon me. I come here for seclusion from my family and friends for five or six months of the year, and do all of my actual writing in that period. Then I return to my family in Nebraska,

Colorado, and New Mexico with no thought of work. This is a period of relaxation, absorption, and refreshment at the fountain-head of the life I write about. Then I return again to my task, systematically. I work as a pianist practises, who does his daily stint just as he takes his bath or breakfast. This enables me to achieve a great deal in a comparatively short period. Of course I don't publish everything that I write. Sometimes the Lord gives us grace to tear up and destroy."

A portrait on the wall of George Sand by Couture, done in the lithographic medium that I was employing, turned our talk to artists of the brush and pencil. The Impressionists take a high place in Miss Cather's predilections, Manet standing out, for her, above them all. Among contemporary Frenchmen the powerful Forain spells for her only horror and brutality. I was amazed at her accurate memory of the pictures in the Commondo collection in the Louvre. Each canvas seemed indelibly stamped upon her memory; my own was put to shame even though these rooms were a favorite haunt of mine. I should have been warned by this when later we argued about the authorship of a picture that I have known for twenty years, a work of Tintoretto, the original of which I had seen in the Doge's Palace rather recently in the same room with some paintings of Veronese. Being a bit less robust in treatment than the former master's usual manner, I attributed it to the latter, persisting despite Miss Cather's objection. A wager was the outcome of the argument, payment proceeding promptly to my antagonist when a book on Tintoretto had heaped upon me chagrin for my fickle memory.

Menace to Culture in Cinema and Radio Seen by Miss Cather

Brunswick, Me., May 14—Willa Cather, whom critics have accorded a rare place as technician and artist in the field of the novel, reluctantly discussed technique in the novel here last evening before the Institute of Modern Literature. Reluctantly because she is a novelist who believes that there has already been too much talk about technique, who says that the only place where she never hears any discussion of it, any suggestion that such a thing actually exists, is among writers, and that therefore she felt she might not bring to the subject such sympathy and knowledge as has been expected of her.

Professor Frederick Brown introduced Miss Cather, whose lecture was arranged by the generosity of the Society of Bowdoin Women. Professor Brown paid tribute to Miss Cather's unremitting effort in editing the Mayflower Edition of the poems of Sarah Orne Jewett, upon whom Bowdoin College conferred an honorary degree, and identified Miss Jewett as Miss Cather's literary mentor. Professor Brown felt that the upholding of a sound and beautiful tradition in American letters had been in considerable measure due to Miss Cather.

Miss Cather did not proceed with her formal talk until she had paid tribute to Miss Jewett. "I want to confirm the saying of Professor Brown as to my purpose in coming here," she said. "Longfellow and Hawthorne, whose commencement anniversaries you celebrate, did not bring me here. After all, Longfellow and Hawthorne both undoubtedly had good credits, and, therefore, they had to graduate from Bowdoin College. But this institution did not have to confer a degree upon Sarah Orne Jewett, so fine an artist, among the foremost in this country. And by conferring the degree Bowdoin College placed itself

This article originally appeared in the 14 May 1925 *Christian Science Monitor* and is reprinted from *Willa Cather in Person: Interviews, Speeches, and Letters,* selected and edited by L. Brent Bohlke (Lincoln: University of Nebraska Press, 1986), 154–57. © 1986 by the University of Nebraska Press. Reprinted by permission of the University of Nebraska Press.

irrevocably on the side of the highest tradition in American letters. I have come, therefore, to express my gratitude to Bowdoin College."

There was a space of silence. Sarah Orne Jewett's friends were in the audience. Her sister was there. Maine knew and loved Miss Jewett, and the institute paid her thus its tribute of honor and grateful memory.

Miss Cather took up her subject:

The subject is so big that the best thing to do would be to wish you goodnight and not speak at all. On the novel in general I have rather pessimistic views, I think. I sometimes think the modern novel, the cinema, and the radio form an equal menace to human culture. The novel has resolved into a human convenience to be bought and thrown away at the end of a journey. The cinema has had an almost devastating effect on the theater. Playwriting goes on about as well as usual, but the cheap and easy substitutes for art are the enemies of art. Illiteracy was never an enemy of art. In the old days all forms of literature appealed to the small select audiences. I tried to get Longfellow's *Golden Legend* in Portland this afternoon to send away to my niece. The bookseller said he didn't have it and would not sell it if he did. He said he was cutting out all his two dollar books because people wanted Zane Grey and such.

At its best the novel has warmth and nearness to us all. Perhaps the novel has become too democratic, too easy to write. The language of the novel is a common language, known to everyone. Among fifty friends there may be many who know they have not much culture in music or art, but if your friends are like mine every one of such a number believes himself a final authority on the novel and quite capable, if he had a minute, to sit down and write one.

Back in the beginning of art, when art was intertwined inseparably with religion, there had to be great preparation for its ceremonials. The creature who hoped for an uplifted moment often endured privation in preparation for that moment. I do not think we should sit at home, in the clothes in which we have been working all day, and turn on the radio to hear the Boston Symphony. I think something more than passivity should be expected of the recipient of any such bounty as Brahms.

There is much talk in the critical magazines and in colleges about the technique of the novel. I never hear the talk among writers. Sometimes I think it is something the critics invented for the sake of argument. Of course there are several things that do make up what people mean by "technique," this thing about which young professors talk so much.

I suppose plot is a part of technique. There are two kinds of novel writing. One affects the plot a lot, the other not at all. Critics and teachers, I think, do not realize that they often pull one kind over into the other. Shakespeare thought so little of plot that he never made one, but even in him there is always a spiritual plot inside the crude, coarse, often violent plot he borrowed from Plutarch or someone else. He never cared where he got his plots. Sometimes the spiritual and crude plots fuse beautifully, as in *Othello*. All the lovely writing in *A Winter's Tale*, on the contrary, is in the pastoral places. It is manifestly wrong to consider plot as an essential part of the novel, when the writer has obviously not considered it.

Then there is characterization. I have found chapters and chapters on characterization in text books intended to be read by young people who did not know how to discriminate between the uses of "which" and "that," iniquitous chapters certain to destroy true skill. Characterization is not an adroit process. It is difficult because it is so simple. The characters we want most to present are the characters whose charm we have felt most strongly.

Hate is a fruitful emotion, but it has not produced great literature. Dante's *Inferno* and the whole *Commedia* is inverted evil, hatred of evil because of the love of good. The great characters in literature are born out of love, often out of some beautiful experience of the writer. There is clumsiness and adroitness in everything. But when I hear speakers telling how characterization was done I feel they are going afar.

Atmosphere was invaluable to the novel before it was called that or had a name. Atmosphere should be felt and not heard. It has been overdone by the method of exploitation. Thomas Hardy understood atmosphere as perhaps few writers have, but Hardy's atmosphere is never obtrusive. It is like the sea on your Maine shore—always there. It is not my intention, however, to abuse my fellow writers.

Another thing we do not hear as much about, but which is very important, is the writer's relation to his material. Not only his emotional, moral, and spiritual relation, but his physical relation to it. The writer of a novel must decide at the outset upon his viewpoint. It is as important as the engineer's deciding on the strain of a bridge. And his relation to it may not constantly change without serious faults of form and coherency. I think there is frequently a too facetious relationship to material. Almost no writer dares write except as if he had something to sell.

Ah, if only there were such a thing as technique. The violinist makes his language by his technique. The actor by his. Pavlowa practices technique each day when she is at sea. I have watched her. . . . But what can the writer do? Pot hooks? Hangers? Here is nothing so valueless as good writing. If he wrote a good book two years ago he cannot go back and write it over. The novel must vary between excitement, which has its value, and that purer beauty which satisfies us like an old Grecian urn. But let us not talk overly about technique which will divest the novel of its best quality. The author who writes to please, not his publisher or the critics, but himself, first comes close, I believe, to what the novel should be. It is not a perfect way, but it is good.

The Novel Démeublé

Willa Cather

The novel, for a long while, has been over-furnished. The property-man has been so busy on its pages, the importance of material objects and their vivid presentation have been so stressed, that we take it for granted whoever can observe, and can write the English language, can write a novel. Often the latter qualification is considered unnecessary. In any discussion of the novel, one must make it clear whether one is talking about the novel as a form of amusement, or as a form of art; since they serve very different purposes and in very different ways. One does not wish the egg one eats for breakfast, or the morning paper, to be made of the stuff of immortality. The novel manufactured to entertain great multitudes of people must be considered exactly like a cheap soap or a cheap perfume, or cheap furniture. Fine quality is a distinct disadvantage in articles made for great numbers of people who do not want quality but quantity, who do not want a thing that "wears," but who want change,—a succession of new things that are quickly threadbare and can be lightly thrown away. Does anyone pretend that if the Woolworth store windows were piled high with Tanagra figurines at ten cents, they could for a moment compete with Kewpie brides in the popular esteem? Amusement is one thing; enjoyment of art is another.

Every writer who is an artist knows that his "power of observation," and his "power of description," form but a low part of his equipment. He must have both, to be sure; but he knows that the most trivial of writers often have a very good observation. Mérimée said in his remarkable essay on Gogol: "L'art de choisir parmi les innombrables traits que nous offre la nature est, après tout, bien plus difficile que celui de les observer avec attention et de les rendre avec exatitude."

There is a popular superstition that "realism" asserts itself in the cataloguing of a great number of material objects, in explaining mechanical processes, the methods of operating manufactories and trades,

From *Willa Cather on Writing: Critical Studies on Writing as an Art* (New York: Alfred A. Knopf, 1949), 35–43. Copyright 1949 by the Executors of the Estate of Willa Cather. Reprinted by permission of Alfred A. Knopf, Inc.

and in minutely and unsparingly describing physical sensations. But is not realism, more than it is anything else, an attitude of mind on the part of the writer toward his material, a vague indication of the sympathy and candour with which he accepts, rather than chooses, his theme? Is the story of a banker who is unfaithful to his wife and who ruins himself by speculation in trying to gratify the caprices of his mistresses, at all reinforced by a masterly exposition of banking, our whole system of credits, the methods of the Stock Exchange? Of course, if the story is thin, these things do reinforce it in a sense,—any amount of red meat thrown into the scale to make the beam dip. But are the banking system and the Stock Exchange worth being written about at all? Have such things any proper place in imaginative art?

The automatic reply to this question is the name of Balzac. Yes, certainly, Balzac tried out the value of literalness in the novel, tried it out to the uttermost, as Wagner did the value of scenic literalness in the music drama. He tried it, too, with the passion of discovery, with the inflamed zest of an unexampled curiosity. If the heat of that furnace could not give hardness and sharpness to material accessories, no other brain will ever do it. To reproduce on paper the actual city of Paris; the houses, the upholstery, the food, the wines, the game of pleasure, the game of business, the game of finance: a stupendous ambition—but, after all, unworthy of an artist. In exactly so far as he succeeded in pouring out on his pages that mass of brick and mortar and furniture and proceedings in bankruptcy, in exactly so far he defeated his end. The things by which he still lives, the types of greed and avarice and ambition and vanity and lost innocence of heart which he created—are as vital today as they were then. But their material surroundings, upon which he expended such labour and pains . . . the eye glides over them. We have had too much of the interior decorator and the "romance of business" since his day. The city he built on paper is already crumbling. Stevenson said he wanted to blue-pencil a great deal of Balzac's "presentation"—and he loved him beyond all modern novelists. But where is the man who could cut one sentence from the stories of Mérimée? And who wants any more detail as to how Carmencita and her fellow factory-girls made cigars? Another sort of novel? Truly. Isn't it a better sort?

In this discussion another great name naturally occurs. Tolstoi was almost as great a lover of material things as Balzac, almost as much interested in the way dishes were cooked, and people were dressed, and houses were furnished. But there is the determining difference:

the clothes, the dishes, the haunting interiors of those old Moscow houses, are always so much a part of the emotions of the people that they are perfectly synthesized; they seem to exist, not so much in the author's mind, as in the emotional penumbra of the characters themselves. When it is fused like this, literalness ceases to be literalness— it is merely part of the experience.

If the novel is a form of imaginative art, it cannot be at the same time a vivid and brilliant form of journalism. Out of the teeming, gleaming stream of the present it must select the eternal material of art. There are hopeful signs that some of the younger writers are trying to break away from mere verisimilitude, and, following the development of modern painting, to interpret imaginatively the material and social investiture of their characters; to present their scene by suggestion rather than by enumeration. The higher processes of art are all processes of simplification. The novelist must learn to write, and then he must unlearn it; just as the modern painter learns to draw, and then learns when utterly to disregard his accomplishment, when to subordinate it to a higher and truer effect. In this direction only, it seems to me, can the novel develop into anything more varied and perfect than all the many novels that have gone before.

One of the very earliest American romances might well serve as a suggestion to later writers. In *The Scarlet Letter* how truly in the spirit of art is the mise-en-scène presented. That drudge, the theme-writing high-school student, could scarcely be sent there for information regarding the manners and dress and interiors of Puritan society. The material investiture of the story is presented as if unconsciously; by the reserved, fastidious hand of an artist, not by the gaudy fingers of a showman or the mechanical industry of a department-store window-dresser. As I remember it, in the twilight melancholy of that book, in its consistent mood, one can scarcely see the actual surroundings of the people; one feels them, rather, in the dusk.

Whatever is felt upon the page without being specifically named there—that, one might say, is created. It is the inexplicable presence of the thing not named, of the overtone divined by the ear but not heard by it, the verbal mood, the emotional aura of the fact or the thing or the deed, that gives high quality to the novel or the drama, as well as to poetry itself.

Literalness, when applied to the presenting of mental reactions and of physical sensations, seems to be no more effective than when it is applied to material things. A novel crowded with physical sensations is no less a catalogue than one crowded with furniture. A book like *The Rainbow* by D. H. Lawrence sharply reminds one how vast a distance lies between emotion and mere sensory reactions. Characters can be almost dehumanized by a laboratory study of the behaviour of their bodily organs under sensory stimuli—can be reduced, indeed, to mere animal pulp. Can one imagine anything more terrible than the story of *Romeo and Juliet* rewritten in prose by D. H. Lawrence?

How wonderful it would be if we could throw all the furniture out of the window; and along with it, all the meaningless reiterations concerning physical sensations, all the tiresome old patterns, and leave the room as bare as the stage of a Greek theatre, or as that house into which the glory of Pentecost descended; leave the scene bare for the play of emotions, great and little—for the nursery tale, no less than the tragedy, is killed by tasteless amplitude. The elder Dumas enunciated a great principle when he said that to make a drama, a man needed one passion, and four walls.

Part 3

THE CRITICS

Introduction

Considering three stories from different periods in Cather's writing career, John J. Murphy, in "Willa Cather's Children of Grace," reminds us of one of Cather's special qualities—her persistent reworking of thematic questions and associations. The motif that Murphy traces here is a Christian one—the effect of a figure endowed with a special grace on the earthbound, or skeptical, recipients of this grace. In the first story, "Jack-a-Boy," published in 1902, the grace-bearer is a child; in the other stories, "The Joy of Nelly Deane," published in 1911, and "The Best Years," Cather's last completed story, this person is a young woman.

Nelly Deane is also the focus of Joan Wylie Hall's article. She concentrates on a different, though not unrelated, symbolic system in "Nordic Mythology in Willa Cather's 'The Joy of Nelly Deane,'" finding that Cather has structured her story on the Norse myth of Idun, the goddess of youth, who, like Proserpine or Eurydice, is associated with spring and renewal. Her account of this story, together with Murphy's, testifies to the intricate patterning so often underlying Cather's simple surfaces.

In her discussion of "Coming, Aphrodite!" Alice Hall Petry links the artist Don Hedger to his dog, Caesar III, to explicate Cather's beliefs concerning "creative endeavor and the place of the artist in society." The ultimatum that the dog appears to deliver his master turns on the question of whether the artist's vocation is absolute. This is a question Cather raises repeatedly in her early stories.

I found selecting from among Marilyn Arnold's many fine readings of Cather's stories difficult in the extreme. I finally settled on her analysis of "Uncle Valentine" because this story remains one of Cather's least discussed and because Arnold traces its delicate effects with a sure hand.

In her book on Cather's romanticism, *The Voyage Perilous*, Susan Rosowski has the good sense to treat the stories of *The Troll Garden* and *Obscure Destinies* as coequal with the novels in significance for understanding Cather's aesthetic. I have chosen to reprint her chapter on *Obscure Destinies* in its entirety; it is the most unified and careful treatment yet given these three important stories.

John J. Murphy

One forgets, during these days of sexual biographies of her, the religious dimensions of Willa Cather's fiction; just as one forgets the largely untapped treasury of short stories she left us—at least ten of which should be included in any list of major American short fiction. This paper might serve as a reminder of both these areas, for its focus is three highly individual stories from different stages of Cather's career, having a common religious theme—that of God's grace operating through children and bringing people together in family. From her twenties to her death, Cather was preoccupied with this theme, which puts her firmly in the tradition of Hawthorne and James in American literature and beyond them in the tradition of inspirational writing that includes Isaiah 7:14: "Behold, a virgin shall conceive and bear a son, and shall call his name Emmanuel [God with us]."

The first story, "Jack-a-Boy" (*Saturday Evening Post*, 30 March 1901),[1] tells in fin de siècle style, like a Beardsley drawing, of an extraordinary child who comes to live in a boarding house and transforms the futile lives of the boarders. Based on Willa's baby brother Jack (John E. Cather, born 1892),[2] the title character, befitting a child of grace, is precocious and androgynous in nature (311), which explains his appeal to both sexes and his instinctive musical talent and response to literary classics.

His initial reception at the boarding house is decidedly hostile, however. These boarders—the spinster music teacher narrator, an old professor preoccupied with dead languages, a decayed beauty of shady reputation, and a spinster landlady who terrorizes her lodgers—are "not . . . those who made the most brilliant success in life" and do not want to be disturbed by a romping child (311). "When Jack-a-Boy came," explains the narrator, "we all eyed him sourly enough, and if looks could kill, the florist would have been sending white roses up to

"Willa Cather's Children of Grace," *Willa Cather Pioneer Memorial Newsletter* 28, no. 3 (Summer 1984). Reprinted with permission of the editor, Mildred R. Bennett.

Number 324" (311). But it is not as expected; the boy's dove-gray eyes and clear treble voice quickly ingratiate him to the boarders. The eyes make the narrator "remember things you had not thought of in years" (311), the very power that restores this tired group to the human family. The Professor emerges from the dusty paraphernalia (including a mummy) of his studies, is reborn as a result of the child's visits to the cluttered room, falls in love with him, and buys jonquils and violets for his May basket because "[t]he yellow ones are gay, like him, and—and I think the violets are rather like his eyes" (317). The narrator reflects that probably the old man "had never said that of a woman's eyes" (317). She also responds to the boy as to a lover, plays for him in the twilight and is moved by the sad melodies he picks out on her piano, "so graceful and individual that they made those hours sweet to remember" (314–15).

She claims after the child's death that it was "his dear little body . . . the little human boy that I loved" (320), but the Professor sees further, that "this was not a human child, but one of the immortal children of Greek fable made flesh for a little while" (318). "No," he tells her, it was not the body she loved, "no, it was the soul" (320). But the Professor cannot see beyond the pagan fables of his scholarship—that the classical divinities occasionally reveal themselves in children—not beyond Pater's idea that "it is the revelation of beauty which is to be our redemption, after all" (322). The narrator remains as limited by her romantic nature theory—"that Jack-a-Boy heard the pipes of Pan as the old wood gods trooped by . . . and that he could not stay" (320)—until the Woman Nobody Called On offers silent testimony to Jack-a-Boy as a child of grace.

The narrator had wondered, considering art forms, "what form of expression the beautiful little soul of his would choose" (315). But the example of the opulent, faded beauty—distrusted and never called on but by Jack-a-Boy, whom she comforts because he feels her love for him exuding from her embracing arms (319)—substitutes a different kind of expression. Less inhibited than the others in showing her affections—from the bon bons she rations him to bringing flowers to his grave (where the Professor and the narrator discover her on May Day)—it is the faded beauty who occasions the narrator's acceptance of the offered grace—the narrator's resolve to call on this ostracized woman—which reveals Jack-a-Boy's full significance as well as the form of expression his beautiful soul will take:

I was thinking how the revelation of the greatest Revealer drew men together. How the fishermen left their nets, without questioning, to follow Him; and how Nicodemus, who thought himself learned, came to Him secretly by night, and Mary, of Magdala, at the public feast, wiped his feet with her hair. (322)

A decade later "The Joy of Nelly Deane" (*Century*, October 1911)[3] depicted a more complex revelation of God's grace through a child (a high school chum) to a hesitant narrator. The story opens before a performance of Bradbury's Queen Esther cantata with Nelly Deane in the title role and being fussed over by three doting Baptist matriarchs. Like Esther, Nelly's beauty and charm are a source of light.[4] Just as the biblical heroine saved her people from destruction, Nelly enables the folk, especially the women, for miles around Riverbend, Nebraska, to survive life's difficulties. Nelly's foil, narrator Peggy, notes that the matriarchs loved Nell differently than they did their own daughters and watched over her as over a blossoming century plant: "I think they loved her for her unquenchable joy" (56).

Where Jack-a-Boy is precocious, Nelly is spoiled. She is a mixture of the praiseworthy and naughty, her foolhardiness and waywardness contributing as much to her joy as her beauty and charm do. She has her own way with her permissive parents, who spoil her with whipped cream tarts and extravagant clothing they cannot really afford; but she has difficulty with the discipline demanded at the local high school. Narrator Peggy notes that while the dear old matriarchs loved Nelly for what she was, they were bent on "looking for influences to change her" (57). Their very names suggest their contradictory responses to the girl: Dow means fading, Spinny indicates enclosure with thorns, and Freeze implies hardness as well as lack of warmth. Nell represents what each has lost, forbidden in her own children, yet must respond to because it brightens life. There is a feminist angle to this, in that joy-killing husbands have in each case stifled what Nell has come to represent. The little white bower of Nell's girlhood, "flooded all day long with sunlight from east and south windows that had climbing roses all about them in summer" (60), recalls Phoebe's room in *The House of the Seven Gables*. But the story goes beyond the narrow, sexist view. Two hymns Nell sings, "The Ninety and Nine" and "There is a Green Hill," reflect a more universal ambivalence: Nell is both lost sheep and bringer of the glad tidings of Christ's redemption.

Like the spinster piano teacher in "Jack-a-Boy," who failed until the end to understand the child's meaning, Peggy, also unmarried and rootless, must see her friend as more than the epitome of girlhood snuffed out by a niggardly male. Matriarch Spinny's son Scott, a bad-mannered hardware merchant, does challenge Nell's waywardness, attempts to protect qualities in her he is unable to appreciate, and successfully traps her in marriage; he does indeed represent the male threat to girlhood, but what it threatened is Peggy herself, the girlhood she prefers to keep inviolate. When Nell tells her of her initial engagement to Guy Franklin, Peggy senses "imminent change and danger" (61); she actually fears the loss of what Nell has become for her—the security of her own maidenhood—and she places a protecting arm over her friend.

The demise of Nell's girlhood is her immersion as a Baptist, a preliminary to her marriage to Scott. Peggy recognizes that the matriarchs have had their way, that the solitary sheep has joined the fold. She equates this baptism, as well as Nell's proposed marriage, with death as she watches Nell lowered beneath the dark water. The maiden bower will now be invaded, but first Peggy must hurry away to Denver, "afraid of what [Nell] might tell me and what I might say" (63). Nell detects her friend's feelings, tells her that "there were some things I would never learn, for all my schooling."

The revelation comes ten years later, when Peggy returns to Riverbend to hear from Mrs. Dow the story of Nell's death after childbirth. At Peggy's suggestion that Nell's death might be due to Scott's neglect rather than God's will, Mrs. Dow protests: "We must just feel that our Lord wanted her *then*, and took her to Himself" (66). The old ladies can accept Nell's passing as inevitable with time, but this is difficult for Peggy. Only when she discovers Nell's spunky eight-year-old daughter out sledding does she recognize the renewal, the perpetuity, of her friend's joy. When she sees the infant boy Nell left behind, the child of her suffering, and the gray heads of the matriarchs bowed over him, she transcends her feminist view, and the joy of Nelly Deane translates into the grace of the Holy Child and the glad tidings of Christ's redemption. As Peggy holds him, haloed by golden fuzz, she senses "the flush of new beginning, of the new morning and the new rose. He seemed to have come so lately from his mother's heart! It was as if I held her youth and all her young joy" (68).

Innocence and grace, suffering and death, and redemption and renewal are central to the last story Cather completed before her death in 1947. "The Best Years," a nostalgic, idealized version of Cather's own childhood family, published posthumously in *The Old Beauty and Others* (1948),[5] includes a description of the long attic room in the Red Cloud house, portraits of her parents, Charles and Virginia Cather, in Mr. and Mrs. Ferguesson, and of her brother Roscoe, between whom and Willa "there never had been the slightest cloud,"[6] in the Ferguesson son Hector. The story captures this family during a special weekend, one of the last times they are all together as a family, a few months before the death of daughter Lesley, who inspires through pure goodness and giving rather than through unrestrained joy or sweet precocity.

Lesley's inspirational and sacrificial nature is evident in her school teaching as well as in her absorption in her brothers, in their blood as in their affections—Hector, for example, has "the fair pink-cheeked complexion which Lesley should have had and didn't" (126). Her scholars are faultless, and when the Illinois boy wets his pants during Superintendent Knightly's visit to Wild Rose schoolhouse, there is "[n]ot a wink, or grin, or even a look" (83). "How do you do it?" asks Miss Knightly, but Lesley does not know, for their goodness is a mysterious consequence of her own. At home, Lesley is "telepathically one" (94) with her brothers; Mrs. Ferguesson delights in her only daughter, and her husband is roused from his usual preoccupations to attend to his daughter and learn the names of her pupils. For Lesley, being among them is like an uprooted plant put "gently back into its own earth with its own group" (96–97).

In the last half of the story a Christmas Eve vignette clarifies this story as yet another Cather parable of grace. Hector makes his way through town in a clumsy new overcoat Lesley has bought him; he recognizes her kindness, the extent to which she puts herself out for others, and he promises himself to show his appreciation someday when he is successful. Then he imagines the first Christmas, wonders if the angels keep the anniversary, and remembers a picture in Lesley's bedroom of angels flying toward the three crosses of Calvary. The joyful family feast is thus transformed into its harsh outcome, that of Christ shedding blood, just as the Ferguesson's perfect happiness is shattered by Lesley's death.

The reader is distanced from the catastrophe; we learn from a friendly railroad conductor the circumstances of Lesley's death as he describes them to Miss Knightly: how the girl saved her scholars by refusing to let them out in a blizzard, how she caught a chill, became delirious and died. Drained through giving, to her scholars and her brothers, "[s]he didn't seem to have strength to rally" (124). Thus ends that pause in time, that happy equilibrium of family living Mrs. Ferguesson later calls the best years.

But the Ferguesson blood thrives; Lesley's brothers are successful in various pursuits of science, farming and business, and they return periodically to visit her grave, as pilgrims to the shrine of a saint. In death as in life her spirit keeps them a family.

Like Jack-a-Boy and Nelly Deane, Lesley Ferguesson inspires community; the words of the spinster narrator of "Jack-a-Boy" express what all three characters of grace magnify, "the revelation of the greatest Revealer [which] drew men together."

Notes

1. *CSF*, 311–22.

2. Mildred R. Bennett, *The World of Willa Cather* (Lincoln: University of Nebraska Bison Book, 1961), 38, 199.

3. *CSF*, 55–68.

4. Esther 2:7 identifies the Jewish heroine as beautiful and charming; Apocrypha 2:15–16 notes that she charmed all who saw her and equates her with water and light.

5. *OBO*, 75–138.

6. James Woodress, *Willa Cather: Her Life and Art* (New York: Western, 1970), 264–65.

Joan Wylie Hall

Several years ago Bernice Slote complained that Germanic-Norse mythology was "a body of reference that has scarcely been recognized in Willa Cather's work."[1] Cather's probable sources, according to Slote, include Carlyle's *Heroes and Hero Worship*, several of Charles Kingsley's books, Jacob Grimm's *Teutonic Mythology*, and Hamilton Wright Mabie's *Norse Stories*. Slote convincingly relates the account of the world tree Ygdrasil in *Norse Stories* to the description of the Burdens' Christmas tree in *My Ántonia*, and she adds that similar allusions abound in Cather's early nonfiction writings, with their references to "the cold north, the polar seas, the Norns, and the Northmen."[2] Aside from recent discussions of Cather's debt to Kingsley's *The Roman and the Teuton* in *The Troll Garden* (1905), her first short story collection, critical commentary has done little to expand upon Slote's observations.[3] An examination of the Nordic materials in "The Joy of Nelly Deane" (1911) will confirm the need for Cather source studies to look beyond the myths of Greece and Rome.

The most obvious Norse element in the story, the strong presence of three wise women who often ply their needlework, has several times been identified as a reference to the Greek or Roman Fates. Thus Sharon O'Brien describes "the Clotho, Lachesis, and Atropos of the sewing circle watch[ing] over their favorite child, plotting glorious futures for Nelly as they sew 'pretty things' for her."[4] That Cather also intended an allusion to the Scandinavian Norns is suggested by repeated mention of ice and snow and, more significantly, by the women's unusual attention to the baptistry, where they welcome Nelly Deane into the church. For the Norns are not only "wonderful spinners of fate, who weave the thread of every man's life"; they also tend the sacred well that nourishes Ygdrasil: "And every day these Norns sprinkled the tree with the water of life from the Urdar fountain, and so kept it forever green."[5]

"Nordic Mythology in Willa Cather's 'The Joy of Nelly Deane,'" *Studies in Short Fiction* 26, no. 3 (Summer 1989). Reprinted by permission of Newberry College.

124

More explicitly than the Roman Fates, the Norns—as personifications of past, present, and future—are associated with the passage of time. Nelly Deane's friend Peggy, who narrates the story, remarks that Mrs. Dow, Mrs. Spinny, and Mrs. Freeze "watched over her [Nelly] as they did over Mrs. Dow's century plant before it blossomed."[6] Peggy emphasizes the parallel between the girl and the plant that dies after a rare flowering when she says she felt "almost as solicitous and admiring as did Mrs. Dow and Mrs. Spinny. I think even then I must have loved to see her bloom and glow" (57).

Much as Mrs. Spinny's name expresses the Norns' function in weaving the length of a person's life, Mrs. Dow's name can be compared to that of the Norn Urd, who represents the past. One meaning of *dow* is "to fade,"[7] and of the three women Mrs. Dow, who describes the fading of Nelly's youth, is most closely linked to the cycles of a year and a life. After Peggy moves away from Riverbend, Mrs. Dow corresponds with her annually, provoking memories of the past and summarizing the news of preceding months, including Nelly's courtship and unhappy marriage to Mrs. Spinny's son Scott. In Rome, ten years after her last visit to her childhood home, Peggy breaks the seal of "one of Mrs. Dow's long yearly letters" to read of the deaths of Mr. Dow and Nelly Deane, along with reports on "new babies and village improvements" (64). The sad news draws Peggy back to Riverbend, to Mrs. Dow's sitting room, "where the carpet and the wallpaper and the tablecover had all faded into soft, dull colors, and even the chromo of Hagar and Ishmael had been toned to the sobriety of age" (64). The Norns traditionally preside at births, and Mrs. Dow relates that Mrs. Spinny called her and Mrs. Freeze to help with the difficult delivery of Nelly's son, a birth that proved fatal to Nelly, though the ladies "fixed [her] up nicely before she died" (66). At the end of the story, after Peggy meets her namesake, Nelly's daughter, Margaret, the old women proudly bend over the baby boy, who has "the flush of new beginnings, of the new morning and the new rose" (68). Under the watchful guidance of the Norn-like trio, the cycle begins again.

The "three dear guardians" (63) frame the story, but Nelly Deane, too, has an antecedent in Norse mythology. Her name echoes that of Idun, beautiful goddess of youth, who inspired the god of music, Bragi, to sing so sweetly that "even the Norns, those implacable sisters at the foot of the tree, were softened by the melody."[8] Cather transfers the sweet voice to Nelly herself, who becomes the star of the Christmas Eve cantata. Idun's beauty is rivaled by Nelly's: "Every one admitted that Nelly was the prettiest girl in Riverbend, and the gayest—oh, the gayest!" (56).

H. A. Guerber remarks that Idun, like Proserpine or Eurydice, is "a fair personification of spring."[9] In the midst of winter, Nelly, too, is connected with warmer seasons. The high school boys in the cantata chorus send to Denver for flowers for Nelly, and several townspeople add their bouquets. Peggy pictures her bedroom as a vernal chamber: "It was a warm, gay little room, flooded all day long with sunlight from east and south windows that had climbing roses all about them in summer" (60).[10] When Nelly tells Peggy about her engagement to Guy Franklin—"flushing all down over her soft shoulders" (60)—Peggy feels "as I did when I got up early on picnic mornings in summer, and saw the dawn come up in the breathless sky above the river meadows and make all the corn fields golden" (61).

The most dramatic episode in Idun's story, her removal from Asgard, home of the gods, by the storm giant Thiassi with the collaboration of the malicious god Loki, corresponds to Nelly's marriage to Scott Spinny after Guy Franklin abandons her. The god of fire, Loki is associated with steel, flint, and the recovery of Thor's hammer; Scott, his modern avatar, is a hardware merchant. Peggy says Scott's face is "so set and dark that I used to think it very like the castings he sold" (58). Reminiscent of Idun's forced lodging in Thiassi's "barren and desolate home of Thrymheim," where she "pined, grew pale and sad,"[11] is Nelly's illness and decline in the "big new house" to which Scott insists they move "before the plastering was dry" (66). Scott mirrors Thiassi's coldness; Peggy senses "something grim and saturnine about his powerful body and bearded face and his strong, cold hands" (62). Although Idun is rescued from Thrymheim, her tale ends with the withering of Ygdrasil, the drying up of the sacred fountain, and Idun's passage—like Nelly's—"into the dark valley of death."[12]

Emphasizing the "complex and subtle designs" in Cather's fiction, Bernice Slote boldly asserts that her references and symbols become so "understated, absorbed, so smoothly integrated that *The Waste Land*, by comparison, is indeed rough terrain."[13] Richard Giannone's excellent discussion of the music in "The Joy of Nelly Deane" shows just how smoothly Cather integrates Christian allusions.[14] Her weaving of Christian with pagan (Nordic, Greek, and Roman) mythology recalls the intricate achievements not only of Eliot but of the Norns themselves.

Notes

1. Bernice Slote, "First Principles: The Kingdom of Art," in *KA*, 36.
2. Ibid.
3. See, for example, Rosowski, 20–23, and O'Brien, 272, 279. Bernice Slote earlier pointed out Cather's interest in Kingsley's treatment of historic cycles and reprinted the pages of *The Roman and the Teuton* that are most relevant to *The Troll Garden* (*KA*, 93–97, 442–44). Cather used Nordic mythology as early as 1891 in her first significant publication, "Concerning Thomas Carlyle," which she wrote while a student at the University of Nebraska. In the essay, Cather remarks that half of Carlyle's heart "was always in Valhalla" and that he was "always down in the chamber of the fates, at the roots of Ygdrasil, the tree of life, which the Norns water day and night" (*KA*, 423, 424).
4. O'Brien, 374.
5. Hamilton Wright Mabie, *Norse Stories Retold from the Eddas* (1882; New York: Dodd, Mead, 1900), 25, 26.
6. "The Joy of Nelly Deane," in *CSF*, 56; hereafter cited in the text.
7. *Oxford English Dictionary*, s.v. "dow." O'Brien, 374, suggests that Cather borrowed the name from Sarah Orne Jewett's character in "The Flight of Betsey Lane," recalling Jewett's "focus on female friendship," but the *OED* definition establishes a symbolic function for Mrs. Dow that is consonant with the more obvious symbolism of Mrs. Spinny and Mrs. Freeze.
8. Mabie, 198.
9. H. A. Guerber, *Myths of the Northern Lands Narrated with Special Reference to Literature and Art* (New York: American Book Co., 1895), 283.
10. Nelly's "tiny, white fur rug—the only one in Riverbend" (60) can be compared to the white wolfskin that Odin provides to protect Idun from the cold (Guerber, 105).
11. Guerber, 102.
12. Mabie, 198.
13. Slote, 93.
14. Richard Giannone, *Music in Willa Cather's Fiction* (Lincoln: University of Nebraska Press, 1968), 47–50.

Alice Hall Petry

In one of her earliest extant writings, Willa Cather—then perhaps nine years old—characterized the dog as "a very intelligent animal" with a "kind, noble and generous" nature.[1] Devoid of the clichéd adjectives which usually striate grade-school essays about pets (e.g., cuddly, playful), Cather's paean to the dog betokens not simply affection, but awe—a respectful recognition that the dog may be perceived as embodying the highest virtues to which man himself aspires. Something of the same attitude towards dogs is evident in a story which Cather wrote some forty years later: "Coming, Aphrodite!" (*Smart Set*, August, 1920; collected in *Youth and the Bright Medusa*, 1920).[2] This curious tale of Don Hedger, a voyeuristic painter, and his brief fling with the capricious Eden Bower, has generated remarkably little critical attention, with most commentators limiting their discussions to analyses of textual variations between the magazine and book versions of the story, or to the elements of Washington Square "local color" which Cather had first experienced in May of 1906.[3] But "Coming, Aphrodite!" is technically and thematically rich, and nowhere perhaps is this more evident than in Cather's presentation of the painter's dog, "Caesar III," which Bernice Slote has aptly termed "one of the most convincing dogs to trot through any work of fiction."[4] Caesar is more than just "convincing," however. He is vital for our understanding of the story's artist-protagonist, Don Hedger. But on a more profound level, Caesar is the medium through which Cather articulates her personal beliefs in regard to the creative endeavor and the place of the artist in society.

In the opening pages of "Coming, Aphrodite!" Cather insists upon the close relationship between Hedger and his dog Caesar, who live together in his studio apartment on Washington Square. They both thrive in an unusual atmosphere: since the studio has only a Northern

"Caesar and the Artist in Willa Cather's 'Coming, Aphrodite!,'" *Studies in Short Fiction* 23, no. 3 (Winter 1986): 307–13. Reprinted with the permission of Newberry College.

exposure, Hedger "never got a ray of direct sunlight" and likewise Caesar's bed was "in the perpetual dusk" (3), but they are very much at home in the twilight, which is insistently unlike the light-bathed apartment soon to be occupied by the flashy Eden Bower. Hedger and Caesar also prefer each other's company to a striking degree. The man and his dog routinely go out to eat together (6), and Caesar is one of the few individuals (aside from "the janitress and the lame oysterman") to whom Hedger ever speaks (10). But this is far more than a simple case of a reclusive man's being close to his pet, for Hedger and Caesar are so similar in appearance and tastes as virtually to have blurred identities. The two are said to resemble each other physically (Hedger has the "muscular jaws" [15] characteristic of the Boston bull terrier), and they both are partial to the distinctive "musty smell of the old hall carpet" (8) for which the landlady holds Caesar personally responsible. Cather further signifies the blurring of their identities by utilizing unclear antecedents. In the following sentence, for example, the italicized "he" could easily refer to either Hedger or Caesar: "He [Caesar] stood thus, motionless, while Hedger watched the lavender girl go up the steps and through the door of the house in which *he* lived" (8). This blurred identities motif may at first appear "corny" or incidental, but not if one considers the twist which Cather has given it: at the same time that the identities of the man and the dog are consistently blurred, Hedger just as consistently treats Caesar with uncommon deference. A vital passage at the story's opening reveals that whenever the two went for walks,

> Caesar III was invariably fresh and shining. His pink skin showed through his mottled coat, which glistened as if it had just been rubbed with olive oil, and he wore a brass-studded collar, bought at the smartest saddler's. (4)

Hedger routinely gives Caesar a bath in the apartment building's communal tub, using special dog soap and being sure to rub Caesar "into a glow with a heavy towel" (14), and after lunch Hedger and Caesar go for strolls expressly "for the dog's health" (7). The artist's attentions to Caesar cannot be dismissed as matters of hygiene or the whims of an indulgent pet-owner, for Cather is careful to emphasize that the dog fares much better than the master: the same man who bought the animal an "elegant collar" (6) at "the smartest saddler's" is himself decidedly shabby:

> Hedger, as often as not, was hunched up in an old striped blanket coat, with a shapeless felt hat pulled over his bushy hair, wearing black shoes that had become grey, or brown ones that had become black, and he never put on gloves unless the day was biting cold. (4)

Further, Hedger clearly is not joking when he reveals that the much-bathed Caesar is doubtlessly cleaner than he is himself (15). What all of this suggests is that Hedger comforts, nurtures, indeed almost worships the dog as if it were the single most important thing in his existence. And because at this pre–Eden Bower stage of the story Hedger is a happily productive artist, it would appear that Cather is positing Caesar as not simply a dog, but as the symbol—more precisely, the incarnation—of what is *really* the single most important thing in Hedger's existence: his artistic sensibility. As shall be seen, the rather fanciful identification of Caesar with Hedger's artistic talents and imagination becomes insistent in the course of "Coming, Aphrodite!" And as a result of that identification, Cather is able to use Hedger's changing attitude towards and treatment of the dog as the story's most sensitive indicator of the degree to which the painter is—or is not—being faithful to his artistic ideals.

Caesar's special status as the embodiment of Hedger's artistic sensibility is particularly apparent in Cather's description of the painter's work habits just before the arrival of Eden Bower. This early in the story, the happily productive Hedger "was painting eight hours a day . . . and only went out to hunt for food" (13):

> When he was working well he did not notice anything much. The morning paper lay before his door until he reached out for his milk bottle, then he kicked the sheet inside and it lay on the floor until evening. Sometimes he read it and sometimes he did not. He forgot there was anything of importance going on in the world outside of his third floor studio. Nobody had ever taught him that he ought to be interested in other people; in the Pittsburgh steel strike, in the Fresh Air Fund, in the scandal about the Babies' Hospital. A grey wolf, living in a Wyoming canyon, would hardly have been less concerned about these things than was Don Hedger. (13–14)

The insistently canine references to the wolf and the "hunt" for food—a phrase reminiscent of "he and his master went out to prowl!" (4)—confirm the close symbolic relationship between the dog and the artis-

tic endeavor. That relationship is further evidenced when Caesar—
even before Hedger—immediately responds negatively to the newly
arrived Eden Bower, the superficial but seductive would-be singer
who disrupts their existence by moving into the adjoining apartment.
Caesar's instinctive distrust of her is palpable: "Caesar was smelling
along the crack under the bolted doors" separating Hedger's studio
from Eden's apartment; "his bony tail stuck out hard as a hickory
withe, and the hair was standing up about his elegant collar" (6). The
naive Hedger, who at this juncture regards Eden more as an inconve-
nient sharer of the communal bathroom than as a threat to his artistic
integrity, tries to placate Caesar by saying, "'You'll soon get used to a
new smell'" (6)—Eden's trademark lilac fragrance. But Caesar's in-
stinctual hostility towards Eden is only confirmed when he scrutinizes
her more closely:

> Caesar stealthily approached her and sniffed at the hem of her lav-
> ender skirt, then . . . he ran back to his master and lifted a face full
> of emotion and alarm, his lower lip twitching under his sharp white
> teeth and his hazel eyes pointed with a very definite discovery. (8)

Like an inarticulate guardian angel, Caesar tries desperately to warn
Hedger against Eden, but to no avail. The painter becomes a voyeur,
daily watching the nude Eden perform calisthenics through a knothole
in his closet wall: "The pull of that aperture was stronger than his
will,—and he had always considered his will the strongest thing about
him" (20). Caesar realizes far better than Hedger that the painter is in
danger: as his master secretly watches Eden, Caesar "would come and
tug at his sleeve, knowing that something was wrong" (20). The dog's
worst fears are confirmed as Hedger, obsessed with Eden, abandons
his work as an artist:

> He was not painting at all now. This thing, whatever it was, drank
> him up as ideas had sometimes done, and he sank into a stupor of
> idleness as deep and dark as the stupor of work. He could not un-
> derstand it. (21)

What Hedger fails to recognize is that the artist's vocation is absolute.
As Cather herself believed, the truly creative individual cannot give
himself entirely both to art *and* to an intense (read "sexual") relationship with another person.[5] Part of the price one must pay to pursue the
artistic vision is the "denial of human relationships and their impact,"[6]

and this is why Hedger—now as completely obsessed with Eden as he formerly was with his art—can no longer paint. Significantly, Eden herself understands this all-or-nothing phenomenon, for she reacts as negatively to Caesar as the dog does to her. When first she meets Hedger and Caesar, she immediately labels the dog's bath sessions "'an outrage': 'I've found his hair in the tub, and I've smelled a doggy smell'" (14). Eden sees clearly that Caesar is hostile towards her: "'You can't move but he's after you. He always makes a face at me when I meet him in the hall, and shows his nasty little teeth as if he wanted to bite me'" (27). Indeed he does; and it is the mutual hostility between Eden and Caesar which results in her ultimatum to Hedger: she will accompany him to Coney Island only "'if you'll leave *that* [Caesar] at home,'" a remark the dog listens to with "flickering ears" (34, emphasis added). As is signified by the "that," a word more appropriate for an abstraction than living thing, this is a power struggle between the carnal and the artistic aspects of Hedger's nature.[7] Eden is quite correct that Hedger "couldn't take both of them" (34), as he must choose between the glittering, sensual, but superficial life offered by Eden, and the more disciplined, ascetic, but satisfying life represented by Caesar. For the nonce, the seductive Eden wins out, as she goes with Hedger to Coney Island and, clad in tights, dangles herself alluringly from a hot-air balloon.

But Caesar, left at home, does not give up the struggle readily. When Eden ascends that night to the roof where Hedger often sleeps, she encounters Caesar, who Argus-like tries to protect his master from her:

> Her foot touched something soft; she heard a low growl, and on the instant Caesar's sharp little teeth caught her ankle and waited. His breath was like steam on her leg. Nobody had ever intruded upon his roof before, and he panted for the movement or the word that would let him spring his jaw. (48)

That signal never comes: "Instead, Hedger's hand seized his throat" (48). When earlier Hedger had watched Eden through the knothole, he would stifle Caesar's warning whine ("those strong hands closed about his throat" [20]); but the rooftop rendezvous provokes Hedger's most aggressive act against Caesar: dragging the dog down from the roof, he canes him "unmercifully" (48). In order to embark on an intense sexual relationship with Eden—in short, to indulge the carnal side of his nature—Hedger must violently repress his artistic sensibility, graphically symbolized by the beating of Caesar.

That Caesar fights no more for Hedger after this incident simply confirms what the beating suggests: that Hedger had *actively chosen* to reject Caesar and the artistic sensibility which the dog represents. Although that sensibility is, as the dog's name indicates, a powerful element in the psyche of the artist,[8] it cannot *force* an unreceptive artist to acknowledge it. Indeed, in and of itself the artistic sensibility has no substance: to be viable, it depends upon the artist just as surely as the artist depends upon it in order to be productive. The relationship is, in a word, symbiotic. This interdependence of the artistic sensibility and the artist is evident early in the story, as Hedger's life consists only of his art and his careful nurturing of Caesar; but nowhere is it more apparent than in the revelation that Hedger literally must carry Caesar to the roof:

> [Hedger] mounted with Caesar under his left arm. The dog had never learned to climb a perpendicular ladder, and never did he feel so much his master's greatness and his own dependence upon him, as when he crept under his arm for this perilous ascent. (11).

After the beating incident and the rejection it symbolizes, Caesar effectively disappears from the story; but fortunately Hedger's relationship with Eden is short-lived. Having quarrelled with Eden over what constitutes artistic "success"—she urges him to emulate a commercially successful artist, Burton Ives, who "'has a Japanese servant and a wine cellar, and keeps a riding horse'" (52)—Hedger leaves town accompanied significantly, by the long-suffering Caesar. When last we see Hedger he has, in a manner of speaking, come to his senses:

> Now it was over. He turned out the light and sat down on his painter's stool before the big window. Caesar, on the floor beside him, rested his head on his master's knee. We must leave Hedger thus, sitting in his tank with his dog, looking up at the stars. (59)

The association of Hedger and Caesar with the stars is significant. Of course stars traditionally betoken a striving for success (*per aspera ad astra*), but they also confirm the reconciliation between man (artist) and dog (artistic sensibility) suggested by the body language of the quoted passage. It was, after all, in that most celestial of locales, the rooftop, that the productive Hedger and the contented Caesar slept before the coming of Eden. So it should come as no surprise to find that eighteen years later Hedger, having striven for stars in the company of Caesar,[9] has achieved fame as an artist, and on his own terms: "'He is one of the first men among the moderns'" (62).

There seems little doubt that Cather intended Caesar to symbolize Hedger's artistic sensibility, but one may reasonably question why she chose a dog instead of a more traditional, ethereal symbol, such as the butterfly in Hawthorne's "The Artist of the Beautiful." Part of the answer may be that dogs are noted for fidelity: no matter how savagely Hedger treated him, Caesar remained loyal to him. In the same fashion, the artistic sensibility—however savagely it may be repressed—will always exist (even if dormant) in the true artist, and it can be nurtured back if the creative individual decides truly to dedicate his life to art. By the same token, dogs traditionally attempt to guard their masters from hostile forces, a role for which they are particularly well-suited by virtue not only of their fidelity but also their ferocity and extraordinary sense of smell. As has been noted, Caesar clearly displays all these qualities, but it is the dog's remarkable sense of smell which Cather most emphasizes as Caesar desperately attempts to protect not Hedger's property, but his artistic integrity. Since Caesar is the incarnation of a mysterious, intangible force deep within the painter's psyche, it is only fitting that Cather emphasize the dog's equally mysterious, intangible sense of smell, which detects not only Eden, but also the threat to Hedger's artistry which she represents. The dog's muteness is closely aligned with this. Caesar acts on instinct: he literally can neither rationalize nor explain how he detects Eden is a hostile force, any more than Hedger could rationalize or explain the creative process. It is further appropriate that Hedger's artistic sensibility be symbolized by a dog because dogs are more conducive to anthropomorphizing than, say butterflies—a fact which makes more tenable the aforementioned blurring of the identities of Hedger (human) and Caesar (canine). That blurring is designed to suggest the uniqueness of the creative act. That is to say, if indeed he is faithful to his artistic integrity, it should be impossible to differentiate between the truly creative individual and his own artistic sensibility:[10] it is part of his own being. The anthropomorphizing of dogs, and in particular of Caesar, is vital for another reason. The bull terrier Caesar is given a "surly disposition": "he had been bred to the point where it told on his nerves"

(4). This is closely aligned with the anti-social behavior and "high-strung" temperament stereotypically attributed to artists,[11] qualities which have led to the labeling of many artists (and dogs) as "mad."[12] Further, the anthropomorphized Caesar is said to be "jealous" of Hedger's attentions "to anyone else" (34). The jealous insistence that the artist devote himself entirely to art calls to mind Yahweh, the "jealous" God of the Old Testament, and in fact Cather once noted that "in the kingdom of art there is no God, but one God, and his service is so exacting that there are few men born of women who are strong enough to take the vows."[13] As Philip Gerber remarks, Hedger's undoing was his turning away from the god of art to join Eden in kneeling to false idols[14]—a turning away signified by the rejection of the dog. In the final analysis, all of these factors in Cather's decision to use a dog as the embodiment of the artistic sensibility hearken back to what she evidently realized even at the age of nine: that the dog is truly awe-inspiring in its nobility, sensitivity, dedication, and faithfulness. So too is the true artist.

Notes

1. Quoted in Bennett, 196.
2. "Coming, Aphrodite!" originally appeared under the title of "Coming, Eden Bower!" in *Smart Set* 92 (August 1920): 3–25. In addition to the title change, the magazine version was quite bowdlerized. For a listing of the approximately one hundred textual variants, see the Appendix in *UVOS*, 177–81. For all quotations in this essay, I follow the text of "Coming Aphrodite!" in *YBM*, 3–63.
3. See, for example, Woodress, 124.
4. Slote, *UVOS*, xvi.
5. David Stouck, *Willa Cather's Imagination* (Lincoln: University of Nebraska Press, 1975), 206. Stouck argues that later in her career, Cather came to perceive "her lifetime dedication to art as placing selfish limitations on life, particularly on human relationships" (207).
6. John H. Randall III, *The Landscape and the Looking Glass: Willa Cather's Search for Value* (Boston: Houghton Mifflin, 1960), 52–53.
7. In this respect, I disagree with David Stouck that Hedger and Eden are "equally matched couples" who "struggle for mastery" (20). It is essentially Caesar, not Hedger, who struggles with Eden.
8. At the same time that the name "Caesar" denotes the power of the artistic sensibility, it suggests the split or break (caesura, cesarian section) in the life of the artist, who must cut himself off from the normal human relationships in order to devote himself completely to his art. In addition, Don

Hedger's dog, Caesar, may call to mind another fictional dog named Caesar: that of Louisa Ellis, the protagonist of Mary E. Wilkins Freeman's short story "A New England Nun" (*Harper's Bazaar*, 1887; collected, 1891). As with Hedger and Caesar, Louisa and her Caesar live happily by themselves and have begun to acquire similarities (she is like a "nun" while the dog is a "hermit"; both eat small, bland meals). As in "Coming Aphrodite!," Louisa's life is seriously disrupted by the arrival of her fiancé, who has been in Australia making his fortune for the previous fifteen years; but with the breaking off of the engagement and his departure, Louisa contentedly reverts to her previous lifestyle. Interestingly, Freeman uses the dog to convey the turmoil in Louisa's subconscious in much the same way that Cather uses Caesar to suggest the degree to which Hedger is compromising his artistic integrity. Particularly striking is Louisa's insistence that the harmless old dog be chained up, an element that may indicate Louisa's determination to repress her own sexuality. (For an excellent analysis of Freeman's story, see David H. Hirsch, "Subdued Meaning in 'A New England Nun,'" *Studies in Short Fiction* 2 [Winter 1965]: 124–36.) Although I have found no concrete evidence that Cather knew Freeman's work, it is difficult to believe that she would have been unaware of the fellow regionalist—and rival to her friend Sarah Orne Jewett—who had managed to achieve what Cather longed for through years as a journalist, editor, and teacher: financial and artistic independence as a fiction writer. Freeman's influence on Cather's work is a very real possibility.

9. Hedger's rise to the front ranks of the modern artists involved many years of hard work—at least four years in the Washington Square apartment before the story opened (3), and eighteen more years after Eden's departure (60). The amount of time involved may explain why the dog's name is Caesar III: he is one of a succession of dogs (all named Caesar) who have accompanied Hedger on the road to artistic success. The abstraction that the dogs symbolize (artistic sensibility) is a stable entity; hence they all have the same name. But the physical dogs themselves do die; hence the numbering system to differentiate among them.

10. The artistic paradox was eloquently expressed by William Butler Yeats in "Among School Children": "O body swayed to music, O brightening glance, / How can we know the dancer from the dance?" (lines 63–64).

11. Cather herself is frequently characterized as being rather cold and unsociable. John H. Randall, for example, summed up her personality by stating that "the most striking thing about her is her insistence on complete self-sufficiency and self-reliance. The next most striking thing is her sense of loneliness and alienation, her apparent necessity to reject for fear of being rejected." Randall goes on to hypothesize that Cather "remained all her life in a permanent emotional state of adolescent rebelliousness" (18). Nonetheless, Randall is able to detect the wistfulness and uncertainty underlying her self-assertiveness (14), and Cather's most recent biographer, Phyllis C. Robinson,

seems to have made a conscious effort to probe Cather's warmer relationships (*Willa: The Life of Willa Cather* [Garden City, New York: Doubleday, 1983]).

12. Cather had "no doubts about the normative reactions to unprecedented behavior. Society in self-justification . . . chooses to regard the artist as mad" (Edward A. Bloom and Lillian D. Bloom, *Willa Cather's Gift of Sympathy* [Carbondale: Southern Illinois University Press, 1962], 139). Particularly valuable as a discussion of Cather's attitude toward the artist is chapter 4, "The Artistic Chain of Human Endeavor."

13. Cited in Phillip Gerber, *Willa Cather* (Boston: Twayne Publishers, 1975), 69. As a side note, it is difficult to believe that Cather did not notice the dog/god anagram.

14. Gerber, 69.

Marilyn Arnold

Three major novels occupied Cather's time between the publication of "Coming, Aphrodite!" and "Uncle Valentine" (*Woman's Home Companion*, February, March 1925). They are *One of Ours* (1922), *A Lost Lady* (1923), and *The Professor's House* (1925). "Uncle Valentine," as will be seen later, has an important thematic relationship to these novels. Busy as Cather was with longer fiction at this time, she still continued to produce occasional short fiction, much of it of a very high quality. "Uncle Valentine" is one of her richest, most satisfying stories, perhaps because she gives herself to it so completely. She is present in every feeling, setting, mood, and incident.

Cather was not one to forget, and in "Uncle Valentine" she calls up the figure of Ethelbert Nevin, a musician and songwriter whom she had many years earlier described with loving superlatives in several newspaper columns. She knew him well, regarded him as her first bonafide artist friend in Pittsburgh, and spent many happy hours with him and his family at Vineacre in the country outside Pittsburgh. Vineacre (called "Greenacre" in the story) is the setting for "Uncle Valentine," and Valentine Ramsay is drawn from Nevin, who died at age thirty-eight in 1901.[1] Cather's description of Nevin, published in the *Journal*, 24 March 1901, is, to the letter, a portrait of Valentine Ramsay, whom Cather created fictionally in the middle 1920s:

> His personality had preserved all the waywardness, freshness, enthusiasm and painful susceptibility of youth, and he had never become accustomed to the routine processes of living, but found life always as new, as perplexing, as untried, as violent and as full of penetrating experiences as he had found it at eighteen. He had never developed the fortifying calm which usually comes to a man of genius in his thirties, the interior life which goes on undisturbed by external mischances. . . . He had been unable to place any sort

"Pittsburgh and the Conflict of Values: Mixed Melody," in *Willa Cather's Short Fiction* by Marilyn Arnold (Athens: Ohio University Press, 1984), 119–26. Reprinted by permission of the publisher.

of non-conducting medium between the world and himself, no sort of protection to break the jar of things. . . . Every day that he lived he got up to meet life as barehanded and raw to the weather, disturbed by the roughness of the machinery of life, oppressed by the slightest neglect from anyone near him, sensitive to the criticism of strangers, enervated by the gloom of an overcast sky, like a weathervane at the mercy of the uncomprehending and unheeding universe.[2]

"Uncle Valentine" is about the people who lived near Greenacre, Pennsylvania, at the turn of the century, in old country homes as yet untouched by the industrial machine that was steadily snarling toward them. It is about one particular year, one "golden year" (31), in the lives of these people, the year Valentine came home. Having no head for practical matters, as a young man Valentine had allowed himself to be pursued and shackled by the wealthy Janet Oglethorpe, a woman so caught up with spending and owning that he suspects she "bargains in her sleep." After being "dragged about the world for five years in an atmosphere of commonness and meanness and coarseness," he finally ran off with another woman, deliberately creating a scandal, damaging Janet's "pride so openly that she'd have to take action" (13). Valentine's ill-advised and unhappy marriage to a woman of impossible selfishness and stupidity recalls again the similar unfortunate marriages that seem to prevail in Cather's fiction.

One day Valentine comes home to live at Bonnie Brae with the three old men who are quietly wearing out their lives there—his father, the aging but gracious Jonathan; his much older brother, the kindly but somewhat feeble-minded Morton; and his uncle, Jonathan's younger brother, Roland, the child prodigy who came home broken at age twenty-eight and never left again. Next door at Fox Hill are Charlotte Waterford and her husband, Harry, her own four daughters, and two orphaned nieces.

Charlotte, who resembles Mrs. Harling in *My Ántonia*, is one of two remarkable women in the story, and she enjoys an extraordinary friendship with Valentine, a friendship enhanced by her musical background and sensitivity. The other is Louise Ireland, the singer who accommodated Valentine's need to create a scandal in order to free himself from Janet Oglethorpe. Ireland, who combines some qualities of Thea Kronborg, Lucy Gayheart, and Marian Forrester (*A Lost Lady*), appears only in snatches, mainly in Valentine's admiring remarks about her, although the frame story is set in her Paris studio many years after the Valentine story takes place. Ireland's reputation is far from spotless— she had run off with desperate men before—but reputation is often a poor index to personal worth. Valentine describes her as "a glorious creature," insisting that "everything she does is lovely, somehow or other, just as every song she sings is more beautiful than it ever was before." He compares her with Janet: "A woman's behavior may be irreproachable and she herself may be gross—just gross. She may do her duty, and defile everything she touches. And another woman may be erratic, imprudent, self-indulgent if you like, and all the while be— what is it the Bible says? Pure in heart" (14).

To establish the plot line Cather works chronologically through the seasons, as she had done in novels like *O Pioneers!* and *My Ántonia*, letting them set the structural pattern as well as the tone for the story. The year's events, having begun somewhat tentatively in late fall with Valentine's homecoming party, burst into wondrous excursions through forests and over hills with the coming of spring. The experiences of Valentine and his friends next door grow lovelier with the deepening of summer, and Valentine even decides that he just might stay at Bonnie Brae forever. But with the dying summer comes the news that the Wakely property which takes in his beloved woods and meadows has been sold. Worse still, it has been sold to Janet Oglethorpe and her second husband. With Janet closing in on him once more, Valentine cannot stay. After several painful delays, he sails for Europe, and that one glorious year comes to an end. Before two years have passed he is killed by a motor truck outside Louise Ireland's studio.

In one sense, the story's principal character is the narrator, Charlotte's niece Marjorie, because the story chronicles the sixteenth year in Marjorie's life, the year she stands on the borderline between childhood and adulthood. In that crucial year she lives next door to Uncle Valentine, and she will always bear the stamp of that experience. Whether Marjorie's own musical gift flowers is never explicitly stated, but unquestionably her presence in Ireland's studio in the frame story—whether as friend, student, disciple, or casual visitor—is at Valentine's unspoken behest. All those years ago he planted the seed that would one day take Marjorie to Louise Ireland.

Marjorie habitually speaks of "that year" or "that winter" or spring or summer in a way that attaches special significance to it. That year she and Valentine together fend off adulthood, clasp youth and wonder, recreate the Golden Age in their own Arcadian fields. What Cather says of Ethelbert Nevin is true for Valentine: "Indeed it was almost impossible to conceive of his outliving youth, or that there should ever come a winter in his Arcady."[3] Cather had sentimentalized the desire for youth and the Golden Age in early stories like "Jack-a-Boy" and "The Treasure of Far Island," but she avoids sentimentality here because Marjorie and Valentine are aware that the world lies just outside their enchanted gates. It is during that year, too, that Valentine composes his most memorable songs. Marjorie remembers summer as particularly joyous, recalling that she "expected life to be like that forever. The golden year, Aunt Charlotte called it, when I visited her at Fox Hill years afterward" (31).

Clinging to childhood but facing adulthood, Marjorie learns in that year what she will need to know her whole life through. That is the year through which all her sensibilities will filter experience as long as she lives. It sets the standards for sensitivity, for sympathy, for wonder, for pain, for desire, for values that last a lifetime. From Charlotte and Valentine, individually and in combination, she learns the validity of mystery and beauty, and about the importance of place; she learns also about freedom and bondage, and she learns about the essential aloneness of every person. Observing Charlotte and Valentine together, Marjorie comes to understand the meaning of their affection, to understand why Valentine regards Charlotte and Louise Ireland, two women so different from each other, as his best friends. It is because the deepest human attachments are aesthetic; a mutual appreciation of the beautiful is the strongest bond possible. Janet Oglethorpe has to be rejected on the same grounds that Charlotte and Ireland are accepted—aesthetic grounds.

The essential oneness of Charlotte and Valentine is further stressed in their mutual love for the countryside around Greenacre and the houses at Bonnie Brae and Fox Hill, a feeling that is not lost on the perceptive and impressionable Marjorie. Valentine's year in his own place is the most productive year of his creative life, and he is forced to agree with Charlotte when she says, "It's the valley you're tied to. The place is necessary to you, Valentine." Marjorie knows too that "the place was vocal to him. . . . Some artists profit by exile. He was one of those who do not. And his country was not a continent, but a few wooded hills in a river valley, a few old houses and gardens that were home" (31).[4]

Marjorie's lesson on the importance of place is underscored by the almost frantic reactions of the Ramsay and Waterford households to the news that the Wakely place has been sold. She knows that the loss of the creeks and woods means "the end for us" (37). Perhaps nearly as tragic as the loss of place are the terms on which it is lost. Valentine can only interpret it as a loss of freedom and a return to bondage, and Marjorie learns that money in the hands of the stupid or unscrupulous can enslave as surely as any set of chains. Valentine understands Janet's purchase of the Wakely property to be an attempt to gain control over him once more. In despair he cries, "She's Scotch; she couldn't let anything get away—not even me. . . . Everything about her's bunk, except her damned money. That's a fact, and it's got me—it's got me. . . . That was her creek we were playing along this afternoon. . . . I can't get in or out" (36). Thus Valentine is forced to flee again from Janet, whose callous presence is enough to paralyze him. With Greenacre lost, he has little to live for, and in less than two years he is dead.

Crassly materialistic as she is, Janet Oglethorpe is only symbolic of a still larger threat to Greenacre, and even to art itself. The Ramsays have never been taught how to compete in a world run by machines and money, and their fate has been predestined from the time Roland withdrew from the world and came home. The defeat of the Ramsays is assured in the inevitable industrial takeover of their air and lands and streams. Though in the particular year of the story, the characters see the city's industrial smoke as a distant threat at most ("that smoke did not come down to us; our evenings were pure and silvery" [25]), Marjorie reports years later that life at Bonnie Brae as Valentine had conceived it could have lasted only a moment anyway. It was just one weak and ineffectual stay against impossible economic odds. The Hartwell home in "The Namesake" was similarly doomed.[5] Finally, the only thing that remains of Bonnie Brae and Fox Hill is the song Valentine had written about Uncle Harry's retaining wall and the profusion of blood red roses that covered it.

Thus, here too, as she does in so many stories and novels, Cather decries the exploitive materialism that scores lives and destroys landscapes. The settings may be different, but in this thematic concern "Uncle Valentine" bears a special relationship to the three novels of the same period mentioned earlier. In *One of Ours*, Claude Wheeler's love for the land and growing things is posed against his father's lack of feeling for it and his brothers' inordinate interest in profitable business ventures. Nat Wheeler is the kind of man who cuts down a beautiful cherry tree for a joke. Ivy Peters in *A Lost Lady* is almost a male incarnation of Janet Oglethorpe. He takes special pleasure in gaining control of the Forrester property and the woman who had lived there with a style he had no capacity to appreciate. His only concern is to make money off the land. He has no feeling for it. And his kind are on the ascendance; in the wake of their onslaught the land is sucked up, and the old values and beauties crumble. It is detecting the same impulse in his family that finally breaks the spirit of Godfrey St. Peter in *The Professor's House.* In their increasing desire for money and material things, people like Janet Oglethorpe and Ivy Peters participate in the destruction of life's true valuables just as surely as does the collector who carries off Tom Outland's mesa relics.

Another of Cather's favorite themes, individual freedom, also figures in this story. She has always insisted that the freedom to be oneself, to pursue one's loves, to have one's place, unfettered by ugliness or meanness or greed, is one of life's highest values. In "Uncle Valentine" Marjorie learns the importance of freedom very early from Charlotte, and realizes it more fully through Valentine. Charlotte, she remembers, "allowed us a great deal of liberty and demanded her own in return. We were permitted to have our own thoughts and feelings" (9). Marjorie comes to realize that the contempt with which city people viewed Valentine after his scandalous behavior and his inauspicious homecoming was actually envy, "because everything about him told how free he was. And up there, nobody was free. They were imprisoned in their harsh Calvinism, or in their merciless business grind, or in mere apathy—a mortal dullness" (15–16). Perhaps the dominant image in the story, in terms of sheer numbers, is the image of a window, a symbol of freedom.

The kind of privacy and personal freedom so essential to the sensitive human being carries something of a dark corollary, however—the indisputable fact that every human creature on this earth is, finally and essentially, alone. It is a fact which many Cather characters confront: Godfrey St. Peter, Myra Henshawe, Bishop Jean Latour, Sapphira Colbert, to name a few; and it is another of the vital things Marjorie learns in her crucial sixteenth year. One evening after a hike with Valentine she feels intensely aware of the night and "vaguely afraid to be alone" (29). She seeks out Charlotte, but Charlotte sends her off to bed, pleading a headache and a need for solitude. Uncle Harry also puts her off, as does Valentine when she discovers him lying in the study in the moonlight. Walking in the garden alone, still disinclined to sleep, Marjorie hears from the Japanese summerhouse "a groan, not loud, but long, long, as if the unhappiness of a whole lifetime were coming out in one despairing breath." Looking inside, she sees "Roland, his head in his hands, the moonlight on his silver hair." She steals away, realizing that "tonight everyone wanted to be alone with his ghost" (29–30).

Roland is the symbol of that basic human aloneness Cather is describing, and his anguish is a dark tonal thread which runs through the story, muting the happy days, breathing the reality of past sorrow and the threat of future sorrow into the carefree winds of the golden year. Wherever there is music, there is Roland—a shadow at the window, a groan behind the wall, a figure in the doorway, a waxen face at a concert. He had been a prodigy, and now he is lost.

Symbolizing the aloneness of all the characters and their inevitable lostness in the grip of an encroaching materialism they will not be able to withstand, and symbolizing as well the defeat of the artistic sensibility, Roland in a very particular way also spells out Valentine's fate. Returning with mature subtlety to the device she had used ten years earlier in "Consequences," Cather makes Roland the ghost of Valentine's future self. Like Kier Cavenaugh, Valentine is haunted by the self he could become, and the realization is intolerable to him. When Valentine runs from Bonnie Brae to Europe, he is running from his future self, projected before him in Roland, as well as from Janet Oglethorpe. Valentine senses a special relationship between Roland and himself. Commenting on Roland's condition on the night described earlier, Valentine asks a rhetorical question: "Do you suppose that's the way I'll be keeping Christmas ten years from now, Charlotte?" (20). Returning from several days in the city, having decided to remain at Bonnie Brae, Valentine says, "Likely I'm here forever, like Roland and the oak trees" (30). On one occasion he makes an explicit reference to himself and Roland that clearly indicates he is reading his own future whenever he looks at Roland. Valentine says, "What haunts me about Roland is the feeling of kinship. So often it flashes into my mind: 'Yes, I might be struck dumb some day, just like that'" (26). The descriptions of Roland picture a living ghost, a walking corpse, and hence a threat to Valentine in the same way that the old man in the top hat and soiled gloves was a threat to Kier Cavenaugh. Roland has a "waxy, frozen face," motionless features and eyes set in "deep hollows" (23), "just a coffin of a man," Valentine observes. Just as the old man kept appearing in Cavenaugh's quarters, so does Roland keep dogging Valentine's steps. It is not uncommon, Valentine says, for Roland to "come drifting in through the wing and settle himself in my study and sit there half the night without opening his head" (26).

Roland, Valentine, Charlotte, indeed all of them at Bonnie Brae and Fox Hill that year, are particular instruments for Marjorie's education. In creating a legend about Uncle Valentine she learns how important place is, and what freedom means, and what beauty and loneliness are, and what holds people together. Apparently she takes what she has learned to Louise Ireland, the only living being, once life has vanished at Greenacre, whose own schooling guarantees an instant sympathy. Only she and Louise Ireland, in this whole earth, know the meaning of the song casually picked up and casually sung by the young student in Ireland's studio so many years later, the song that begins, "I know a wall where red roses grow . . ."

Notes

1. See *Courier* and *Journal* articles in 1898, 1900, and 1901, reprinted in *WP*, 532–38, 627–42, 650–55, for Cather's tributes to the musician, and for her accounts of personal experiences with him and his family. She wrote in a particularly moving way after his death and funeral. See introduction to *UVOS*, xxiii; Woodress, 89; and Brown, 82, for brief commentary on the relationship between Nevin and Valentine. It has also been suggested that Adriance Hilgarde, the absent musician of "'A Death in the Desert,'" is at least partially drawn from Nevin. Valentine differs from Nevin in one important regard: Nevin's marriage was happy, Valentine's unhappy.

2. *WP*, 638.

3. *Journal*, 24 March 1901. See *WP*, 638.

4. In her feeling for place, Cather is like Valentine. Her personal letters to friends are full of comments about her inability to work except at certain places and under certain conditions.

5. The Hartwell estate to which Lyon Hartwell returned in "The Namesake" is in the same Pennsylvania countryside as Fox Hill and Bonnie Brae.

Susan J. Rosowski

Wonderful things do happen even in the dullest places.[1]

In the decade before *Obscure Destinies* appeared in 1932, it seemed that Willa Cather had turned from Nebraska as resolutely as had her characters Claude Wheeler and Niel Herbert. After *One of Ours* and *A Lost Lady*, she had written novels about other places (Michigan, the Southwest, Quebec), distant times (the mid-nineteenth century, the seventeenth century), and historical people (French priests in New Mexico and immigrants to Canada). But for the three stories included in *Obscure Destinies*, Cather returned to memories of Red Cloud and Webster County. Childhood friends reappear—Annie Pavelka's husband (along with memories of Charles Cather) as the prototype for the Bohemian farmer Anton Rosicky, Grandmother Boak for Mrs. Harris, Margie Anderson for Mandy, Mr. Richardson and Mr. Miner for Mr. Trueman and Mr. Dillon, and young Willa for Vickie Templeton and the narrator of "Two Friends."[2]

Any such identification of prototypes is useful only up to a point, however. In a letter to Carrie Miner Sherwood, Cather wrote that her stories came from emotion, not from the faces and arms and legs of people she knew.[3] And though Cather did return to early materials for her 1932 volume, her emotions about those materials were different from those of *O'Pioneers!* and *My Ántonia*. In her early Nebraska novels Cather's exceptional individuals fulfilled their destinies by rising above the common lot, and her sensitive observers strained to grasp immortal truths in the material world: Alexandra Bergson, to see the beauty of the land; Jim Burden, to see Ántonia as an earth mother; Niel Herbert, to get at the secret of Marian Forrester. Her characters proved their worth by escaping the ordinary—or by attempting to do so; their happiness was, as Jim Burden realized, being "dissolved into something

"Obscure Destinies: Unalterable Realities," in *The Voyage Perilous: Willa Cather's Romanticism* by Susan J. Rosowski (Lincoln: University of Nebraska Press, 1986). © 1986 by the University of Nebraska Press. Reprinted by permission of the University of Nebraska Press.

complete and great."⁴ The phrase echoes in "Neighbour Rosicky," but with an important difference, for in her story of a Bohemian farmer Cather wrote of happiness not in greatness but in a simple life that was "complete and beautiful." Whereas Cather formerly had pulled away to transcend mortality by converting life into art, she now wrote of accepting life as it is.

As so often, Cather's personal life inspired her art. Beginning in late 1927, events revealed the vulnerability of the places and people which youth takes for granted. Within four years Cather lost two homes (she left her Bank Street apartment in 1927; the next year her parents' Red Cloud home was closed) and both her parents (her father suffered a heart attack in 1927, then died in 1928; her mother suffered a stroke in 1928, became increasingly incapacitated durinₑ the next two years, and died in 1931). The two books Cather wrote during this period—*Shadows on the Rock* (1931) and *Obscure Destinies* (1932)—at first glance so different, are thematically complementary: both are about loss, one of home through exile, the other of persons through death. Each contains what the other lacks. In *Shadows on the Rock,* place comes alive, so that Cécile's kitchen seems the living idea of domesticity and the Rock that of faith. By comparison characters seem flat. Because they represent ideas rather than take on lives of their own, they are absolved from the mortal world of change, and death is a distant thing. Madame Auclair is preserved in memory; Euclide Auclair is "scarcely changed at all" by time; Cécile is apotheosized into a Canadian Holy Mother. *Obscure Destinies* is about this subject missing from *Shadows on the Rock.* It is the single volume in Cather's canon about dying (a different subject from death), and it contains Cather's most mature, satisfying treatment of human relationships.

Obscure Destinies opens with a death sentence on its first major character, Anton Rosicky:

> When Doctor Burleigh told neighbour Rosicky he had a bad heart, Rosicky protested.
> "So? No, I guess my heart was always pretty good."

The scientific diagnosis is accurate: within the year Rosicky will die. But the story demonstrates how limited that diagnosis is, and how Rosicky does have a good heart in that which matters—the ability to love. The central tension of "Neighbour Rosicky" involves Rosicky's hunger "to feel sure [his boys] would be here, working this very land, after he was gone," and his fear that his married son, Rudolph, will take a job in the city: "To Rosicky that meant the end of everything for his son. To be a landless man was to be a wage-earner, a slave, all your life; to have nothing, to be nothing." That danger is heightened because the Czech Rudolph has married Polly, an American town girl whose suspicion of country life is evident in her plucked eyebrows, her bobbed hair, and her formal ways with Rudolph's family. "Good evening, Mr. Rosicky," she says when her father-in-law comes. "She never called him father, or Mary mother."

Rosicky cannot stop the drought that is making farming hard for the young couple, nor can he give to them material goods, for he is not a wealthy man. What he has is "a special gift for loving people," offered in quiet, unobtrusive ways. He arranges that Polly and Rudolph will have the family car on Saturday nights; he cleans the kitchen for Polly; he tells of living in London—the most painful time of his life and a subject still so sore it scarcely bears touching—and he does so in English, a "bothersome" language for a long story, so that Polly can hear. Most important, he gives the example of his own contentment.

Cather presents the contentment of her character in the story's slow pace and calm mood. Rosicky quiets those about him by reminding others to talk softly and asking them to withhold questions until after a meal. He slows conversations by drinking coffee from time to time, pausing to take another piece of apple cake, filling his pipe. Alone, he follows the same calm pace. After seeing Polly and Rudolph off to the picture show, Rosicky "took his own time with the dishes. He scoured the pots and pans and put away the milk and swept the kitchen. He put some coal in the stove and shut off the droughts, so the place would be warm for them when they got home late at night. Then he sat down and had a pipe and listened to the clock tick." Simple words and careful details maintain the slow rhythm of the passage. As scenes flow into each other with the same rhythm, their calm seems a preparation for death. After cleaning up at Rudolph's and Polly's, Rosicky walked home and "stopped by the windmill to look up at the frosty winter stars and draw a long breath before he went inside. That kitchen with the shining windows was dear to him; but the sleeping fields and bright stars and the noble darkness were dearer still."

By such pauses Cather presents Rosicky's contentment; by shifting point of view she demonstrates its power. Doctor Ed, a hard-pressed professional who appreciates the welcome of a warm home, pauses to remember breakfast at the Rosickys', and Mary, once a rough farm girl, watches her husband drink coffee and thinks about the gentleness of their life together. These are unconventional materials for fiction, for here important moments are quiet ones when action is suspended, and the most powerful character is one who does little, in the ordinary sense of things. The story's most dramatic scenes occur when action is stopped and Rosicky does nothing. Polly awakens to life while she sits quietly beside her sleeping father-in-law, and Doctor Ed awakens to the beauty about him while he sits silently beside the graveyard where Rosicky lies buried.

Nevertheless, "Neighbour Rosicky" is about power—the power of a man who, like Christ, changes the world by inspiring others to love. Anton Rosicky is a priestly intermediary between flesh and spirit, life and death. Two features, especially, suggest his effect: Rosicky's queer eyes twinkle, so that light surrounds him as if a halo; and his warm touch heals, as if by a laying on of hands. The eyes and the hand, light and warmth, appear in the most casual moments—in the twinkling smile of Rosicky's eyes as he puts more coal in the fire or talks to Mary; in the warmth of his hand as he extends a fee and a handshake to Doctor Ed, an extra ration of oats to his workhorses, an evening in town to Polly. Casual moments, yes, but ones that convey the magical, even sacred power of love. The story's climatic scene is about this power. When Polly sees Anton Rosicky double over in pain, she runs toward him and cries, "Lean on me, Father, hard." In so doing Polly acknowledges Rosicky as her worldly father (shortly thereafter she reveals she is pregnant and, implicitly, will take her place in the Rosicky family) and her spiritual one. When his pain has gone, Polly takes his hand and opens herself to the grace of love:

> His hand pressed hers. She noticed that it was warm again. The twinkle in his yellow-brown eyes seemed to come nearer.
> "I like mighty well to see dat little child, Polly," was all he said. Then he closed his eyes and lay half-smiling. But Polly sat still, thinking hard. She had a sudden feeling that nobody in the world, not her mother, not Rudolph, or anyone, really loved her as much as old Rosicky did. It perplexed her. She sat frowning and trying to puzzle it out. It was as if Rosicky had a special gift for loving people, something that was like an ear for music or an eye for colour. It was quiet, unobtrusive; it was merely there. You saw it in his eyes,— perhaps that was why they were merry. You felt it in his hands, too.

> After he dropped off to sleep, she sat holding his warm, broad, flexible brown hand. She had never seen another in the least like it. . . .
>   Polly remembered that hour long afterwards; it had been like an awakening to her. It seemed to her that she had never learned so much about life from anything as from old Rosicky's hand. It brought her to herself; it communicated some direct and untranslatable message.

Polly's awakening completes the ironic reversal begun in the story's opening exchange: Rosicky dies of a "bad" heart, content in having seen into Polly's good one. His last thoughts are an extended play upon the meanings of "heart," by now used exclusively for the capacity to love: "Girls nowadays didn't wear their heart on their sleeve. . . . Either a woman had that sweetness at her heart or she hadn't. . . . if they had that, everything came out right in the end." Medical distinctions between good and bad hearts are finally irrelevant; as physical organs, all hearts will fail. The important meaning of "heart" concerns the capacity to love, by which continuities are possible—endings with beginnings, one person's dying with new life forming.

Assured about the future of his family, Rosicky feels "the cramp" (not "heart attack") begin again in his chest, and rises, "to get to his bed if he could." Again a play on words presents continuity between life and death, for the bed Rosicky reaches is the grave. As comfortable with death as he was with life, he is ready to rest in "the sleeping fields." Cather prepared for his death by following Rosicky's thoughts as he passed the graveyard, then—something only a highly skilled writer could make work—as he imagined himself lying within it. Upon his death the passage echoes in the reader's mind, as if from the grave Rosicky describes his continuing contentment:

> A man could lie down in the long grass and see the complete arch of the sky over him, hear the wagons go by; in summer the mowing-machine rattled right up to the wire fence. And it was so near home. Over there across the cornstalks his own roof and windmill looked so good to him. . . . it was a comfort to think that he would never have to go farther than the edge of his own hayfield. The snow, falling over his barnyard and the graveyard, seemed to draw things together like. And they were all old neighbours in the graveyard, most of them friends; there was nothing to feel awkward or embarrassed about.

For the conclusion Cather moves outside the Rosicky family to Doctor Ed, who again provides a long perspective. As Polly earlier had sat quietly beside the bed where Rosicky slept, Doctor Ed "stopped his car, shut off the engine, and sat there for a while" by the graveyard where Rosicky lay. Like Polly, Doctor Ed has an awakening:

> A sudden hush had fallen on his soul. Everything here seemed strangely moving and significant, though signifying what, he did not know. Close by the wire fence stood Rosicky's mowing-machine, where one of the boys had been cutting hay that afternoon; his own work-horses had been going up and down there. The new-cut hay perfumed all the night air. The moonlight silvered the long, billowy grass that grew over the graves and hid the fence; the few little evergreens stood out black in it, like shadows in a pool. The sky was very blue and soft, the stars rather faint because the moon was full.
>
> For the first time it struck Doctor Ed that this was really a beautiful graveyard. He thought of city cemeteries; acres of shrubbery and heavy stone, so arranged and lonely and unlike anything in the living world. Cities of the dead, indeed; cities of the forgotten, of the "put away." But this was open and free, this little square of long grass which the wind for ever stirred. Nothing but the sky overhead, and the many-coloured fields running on until they met that sky. The horses worked here in summer; the neighbours passed on their way to town; and over yonder, in the cornfield, Rosicky's own cattle would be eating fodder as winter came on. Nothing could be more undeathlike than this place; nothing could be more right for a man who had helped to do the work of great cities and had always longed for the open country and had got to it at last. Rosicky's life seemed to him complete and beautiful.

In contrast to the quiet, even the stasis, of the previous scenes, this final one bursts with movement—of horses pulling the mowing machine, of new-cut hay perfuming the air, of wind stirring and neighbors passing. And in contrast to the previous focus on one person's life, specifics here join the universal: a little square of grass is "forever stirred" by the wind; one family's fields run into endless sky; a single man has merged with all of nature. This is a graveyard that is part of life, where the fence separating the living from the dead is hidden with grass, where some neighbors lie inside and other neighbors pass on their way to town. "It is not chaos or death—it is form, union, plan—

it is eternal life—it is Happiness": Whitman's words from "Song of Myself" describe Cather's story.[5]

"Neighbour Rosicky" is as Whitmanesque as was *O Pioneers!* In 1913 Cather announced the affinity with her title and then spelled it out with her conclusion—"Fortunate country, that is one day to receive hearts like Alexandra's into its bosom, to give them out again in the yellow wheat, in the rustling corn, in the shining eyes of youth!"[6] In 1928 the affinity is relaxed, natural, unobtrusive—yet nonetheless present as powerfully as ever. Like Whitman, Anton Rosicky bequeathed himself to the dirt to grow from the grass he loved.[7]

In a 1936 essay on Katherine Mansfield, Willa Cather praised the "virtuosity" of Mansfield's short stories, then noted that "it was usually Miss Mansfield's way to approach the major forces of life through comparatively trivial incidents."[8] Cather could have been writing of her own "Old Mrs. Harris," her finest story. It is a simple story, of a woman who has come with her daughter's family from Tennessee to Skyline, Colorado, where she keeps house for them. Here are none of the dramatic incidents of the conventional writer, but instead the seemingly unimportant ones that make up the daily lives of ordinary people: a neighbor brings a coffee cake for Mrs. Harris; a cat dies; the family attends a church supper; fifteen-year-old Vickie wins a scholarship; Victoria Templeton learns she is pregnant; old Mrs. Harris dies. Through such "comparatively trivial incidents," Cather approached "the major forces of life."

The story begins with Mrs. Rosen, the Templetons' cultured, learned Jewish neighbor who tries "to get . . . to the real grandmother" by laying siege to the Templeton home: she spies until she sees Victoria leave, then marches over with her coffee cake to catch Mrs. Harris unaware. But a person can't be "got" that easily. Troubled with the irregular visit, Mrs. Harris is on her guard, and Mrs. Rosen leaves disappointed. The scene establishes the rhythm that continues through the story, between outside and inside, expectation and reality. Before she met the Templetons, Mrs. Rosen was inconsolable, fearing a racket from their children and flies from their livestock; upon coming to know them, she was drawn to their pleasant ways and natural friendliness. She expected Mrs. Templeton as a southern woman to be "willowy or languishing," then found her to be high-spirited, direct, and warmly genuine. She expected the Templeton parlor to be cluttered, then found it neat and comfortable; she expected the Templeton children to be ill-mannered, then found they were most courteous.

Mrs. Rosen's expectations are remarkably similar to a reader's, if my students are representative. Like Mrs. Rosen, these students feel impatience with Vickie, horror at Victoria ("she is a monster," one said), and pity for Mrs. Harris. Yet even as they talk, they move beyond such easy generalizations: someone remarks that the self-centered Vickie is good about minding the baby and thoughtful in buying presents for her brothers; another that the selfish Victoria is loving (she gives her children "a real smile" when she sees them) and generous (without being patronizing, she includes the outcast Maude children in an ice-cream social). And another says that despite her loneliness and her exhaustion, Mrs. Harris is profoundly happy.

By shifting point of view from character to character, Cather maintains this rhythm between outside and inside, expectation and reality. Mrs. Rosen's thoughts about her neighbors are followed by Mrs. Harris's own thoughts, Victoria Templeton's, and Vickie's, until the story resembles a many-faceted gem.[9] The technique resembles that of "Neighbour Rosicky," but its effect is quite different: in "Neighbour Rosicky" points of view come together in a central character, while in "Old Mrs. Harris" individuals seem painfully lonely, each living a secret life which she keeps hidden. Mrs. Rosen does not discuss her sorrow over being childless; Victoria goes into her bedroom and closes the door when she is unhappy; Vickie thinks everyone is an enemy; Mrs. Harris speaks neither of her regret for Tennessee nor of her knowledge she is dying.

Shifting points of view, then, present intensely private lives of very different people; yet even while each individual is solitary, each is part of a family. To read "Old Mrs. Harris" is to experience a double life, "every individual . . . clinging passionately to his individual soul" and, at the same time, participating in a group life.[10] The night Mrs. Harris is dying, we focus upon her, but we know where the others are and what they are feeling: Victoria is in her room, unhappy over her pregnancy; Mr. Templeton is at his farm, where he has enjoyed a chicken dinner and anticipates sleeping in the clean guest bed; Vickie is at her father's office, engrossed in reading; the twins are outside playing with the neighbors; Mrs. Rosen is in Chicago, celebrating her niece's wedding.

Nor surprisingly, the contrasts that are fundamental to "Old Mrs.

Harris"—the expected versus the unexpected, the interior life of an individual versus the group life of the family—produce irony. There are incidental ironies: one woman desperately wishes for children while another desperately wishes she were not again pregnant, and a man moves his family west to improve their fortunes, only to find reduced circumstances. There are humorous ones: Mrs. Rosen's plump body belies her ideal of a responsibly restrained life, and her actions undercut her thoughts (she accepts a second piece of chocolate cake even as she suffers from tightly bound stays and envies Victoria Templeton's figure). Finally, there are the most profound ironies of human existence: people living in a crowded household are lonely; youth is thoughtless and old age solitary; the miracle of life results in the tragedy of death; as one life is ending, another is beginning.

Though individuals in "Old Mrs. Harris" *feel* these ironies, no one understands them. No one has the keen perception of Anton Rosicky; no one experiences awakening as did Polly and Doctor Ed. Sometimes characters turn to the folk wisdom of cliché: "[Life] is not at all fair!" (Mrs. Rosen); "Nothing comes easily in this world" (Vickie); "Life hadn't used her right" (Victoria); "Everything that's alive has got to suffer" (Mrs. Harris). Usually, however, individuals don't articulate truths at all; instead they simply rise above discrepancies by loving generosity. One scene serves as an example. When she sees Victoria Templeton nursing the baby, Mrs. Rosen "could not help admiring him and his mother. They were so comfortable and complete. . . . 'What a beautiful baby!' [Mrs. Rosen] exclaimed from her heart. And he was. A sort of golden baby. His hair was like sunshine, and his long lashes were gold over such gay blue eyes. There seemed to be a gold glow in his soft pink skin, and he had the smile of a cherub." It is a moment of unexpected beauty, in which the woman Mrs. Rosen had thought selfish seems a Madonna with child. And it is one of great generosity—that of a mother feeding her child from her own body, and that of a woman who, bitterly aware she has no children, admires another woman's baby.

Such generosity ignores limitations of age, culture, education, and personality. Victoria regrets her youthful figure and freedom, yet she couldn't resist her twins the moment she saw them, and most surely she will love her new baby as readily. Traditionally southern in her belief that girls should be foolish and romantic, Mrs. Harris cannot comprehend her granddaughter's desire for an education; yet she sees that Vickie has the money to attend the university. Mrs. Rosen is deeply critical of the Templetons' improvident ways, yet she unhesitatingly arranges an unsecured loan to Vickie. Despite their youthful restlessness, the twins sit with their grandmother; and despite her exhaustion, old Mrs. Harris continues to work for her daughter's family. The mystery at the heart of this story is that the family from which individuals are fleeing offers freedom from individuality, and the children who mean unending work for an old woman bring to her youth:

> The moment she heard the children running down the uncarpeted back stairs, she forgot to be low. Indeed, she ceased to be an individual, an old woman with aching feet; she became part of a group, became a relationship. She was drunk up into their freshness when they burst in upon her, telling her about their dreams, explaining their troubles with buttons and shoe-laces and underwear shrunk too small. The tired, solitary old woman Grandmother had been at daybreak vanished; suddenly the morning seemed as important to her as it did to the children, and the mornings ahead stretched out sunshiny, important.

Generosity such as this springs from compassion, from sharing in the suffering of another and giving aid or support; it appears in the most dramatic scene in the story. In the hushed stillness of night and by the soft light of an old lantern, Mandy "performed one of the oldest rites of compassion" by rubbing Mrs. Harris's feet. Less dramatic but similarly significant acts of compassion inform the most ordinary of days. The most powerful scene for me is that of Mrs. Harris's young grandson caring for her as she lay dying. Albert gets a wooden crackerbox as a bedside table, puts a clean napkin on it, pumps water until it runs cold and exchanges the tin cup for a glass tumbler; he then gets one of his linen handkerchiefs for his grandmother, loosens the curtains over the windows, and reads to her. Should Mrs. Rosen have visited her neighbor that night, she undoubtedly would have seen the ordinary objects and mean surroundings as signs of neglect, yet each was an expression for the most tender, thoughtful love. "Grandmother was perfectly happy," Cather wrote of her last hours.

Understanding Mrs. Harris's perfect happiness means putting aside pity and feeling compassion. The distinction is central to the story, one toward which shifts in perspective (expectation and reality, outside and inside) and point of view (Mrs. Rosen, Victoria, Vickie, Mrs. Harris) lead. Pity comes from concern or regret for an inferior, and "to be pitied was the deepest hurt anybody could know." Pity is the outside view of Mrs. Rosen or my students when they judge Victoria selfish and believe Mrs. Harris neglected. Compassion is shared suffering, which means shared humanity, for as Mrs. Harris knows, "Everything that's alive has got to suffer." Compassion means realizing that the narrator, describing youth coming closer to age, includes each of us:

> Thus Mrs. Harris slipped out of the Templetons' story; but Victoria and Vickie had still to go on, to follow the long road that leads through things unguessed at and unforeseeable. When they are old, they will come closer and closer to Grandma Harris. They will think a great deal about her, and remember things they never noticed; and their lot will be more or less like hers. They will regret that they heeded her so little; but they, too, will look into the eager, unseeing eyes of young people and feel themselves alone. They will say to themselves: "I was heartless, because I was young and strong and wanted things so much. But now I know."

"Two Friends" has an even less conventional plot than the other stories in *Obscure Destinies:* a narrator recalls a friendship that ended with a quarrel over politics. But as Cather explained privately, "Two Friends" was not meant to be about the two men at all, but about a picture they conveyed to a child.[11] She indirectly makes the same point in her story. Beginning it, the narrator muses that "even in early youth . . . we yet like to think that there are certain unalterable realities, somewhere at the bottom of things. These anchors may be ideas; but more often they are merely pictures, vivid memories, which in some unaccountable and very personal way give us courage." Seagulls are seemingly free and homeless, yet "at certain seasons even they go back to something they have known before; to remote islands and lonely ledges that are their breeding-grounds." And like the gulls, people too have retreats. "Two Friends" tells of such a retreat that was lost, a picture that was distorted.

"Long ago . . . there lived two friends," in a time as distant as youth is to the adult. Their friendship was exactly contemporary with the narrator's childhood: it began the year she was born; she knew the two men from the time she was ten; she saw them separate when she was thirteen, on the threshold of becoming an adult. In writing her story Cather told how things seemed to her as a child, who didn't notice certain things and exaggerated others, who looked up at her world and, especially, at the two men she admired. R. E. Dillon was the biggest banker of the community and the proprietor of its large general store; he owned farms "up in the grass country." J. H. Trueman was "a big cattleman" with "a high sense of honour," who "was large . . . about money matters." Together they traveled "to big cities" in the wide world beyond their community, and together they represented "an absence of anything mean or small."

Largeness was, it seemed, the one thing the men had in common. They were opposites in almost everything else. Dillon was Irish, Trueman American; Dillon's face was bony and his body wiry, Trueman's face solid and his body heavy; Dillon was a banker and Trueman a cattleman; Dillon lived a regular life, Trueman an irregular one; Dillon talked well, Trueman was usually silent; Dillon was a Democrat, Trueman a Republican. Such differences were unimportant, however, so long as the two men were alike in essentials, both "successful, large-minded men who had made their way in the world when business was still a personal adventure."

To the child who knew them, the friends seemed as constant as nature itself. "Every evening they were both to be found at Dillon's store," in cold weather inside playing checkers, in spring and summer outside in two armchairs. Gestures and rhythms catch their constancy—the poised and resting hands of each man, the cigar that seemed to belong in Mr. Trueman's hand, "like a thumb or finger," the relaxed rhythms of their good talk and the comfortable silences of their friendship.

Details such as these contribute to the picture at the heart of the story: on moonlit summer nights two friends sit outside Dillon's store, a blind wall behind them and a dusty road before them. A simple picture, yes, but something quite remarkable happens in it. By an outpouring of moonlight and silence, sensations melt together—sound, touch, sight, and taste—and then the two men were most "largely and positively themselves." To the child they seemed celestial bodies in space, catching the white light of the moon and casting dark shadows upon earth:

> One could distinguish their features, the stripes on their shirts, the flash of Mr. Dillon's diamond; but their shadows made two dark masses on the white sidewalk. . . . Across the street, which was merely a dusty road, lay an open space. . . . Beyond this space stood a row of frail wooden buildings. . . . These abandoned buildings,

an eyesore by day, melted together into a curious pile in the moon-light, became an immaterial structure of velvet-white and glossy blackness, with here and there a faint smear of blue door, or a tilted patch of sage-green that had once been a shutter.

The road, just in front of the sidewalk where I sat and played jacks, would be ankle-deep in dust, and seemed to drink up the moonlight like folds of velvet. It drank up sound, too; muffled the wagon-wheels and hoof-beats; lay soft and meek like the last residuum of material things,—the soft bottom resting-place.

After such a moment the narrator scarcely needs to explain that "wonderful things do happen even in the dullest places—in the cornfields and the wheatfields." When she goes on to recall, "sitting there on the edge of the sidewalk one summer night, my feet hanging in the warm dust, I saw an occultation," she could be describing the two friends, who "seemed like two bodies held steady by some law of balance, an unconscious relation like that between the earth and the moon." The occultation of Venus that the three saw one night seems a heavenly affirmation of the mysterious balance between the two friends.

That picture of two friends sitting together is one of those "vivid memories" by which we realize "certain unalterable realities, somewhere at the bottom of things"—the purity of high ideas and constancy of large natures. On such memories we rest our faith that if the material world were distilled, its "last residuum" would be not mere matter but an idea. They are "truths we want to keep."

Friendship between the two men ended, however, when Mr. Dillon returned from a Democratic convention afire with the populism of William Jennings Bryan, so simplistically held that a child could grasp it immediately: "that gold had been responsible for most of the miseries and inequalities of the world; that it had always been the club the rich and cunning held over the poor, and that 'the free and unlimited coinage of silver' would remedy all this." History, politics, religion—all combined in arousing emotions about false ideas, based on nothing at all. "Dillon declared that young Mr. Bryan had looked like the patriots of old when he faced and challenged high finance with: 'You shall not press this crown of thorns upon the brow of labour; you shall not crucify mankind upon a cross of gold.'" High-sounding phrases that, when examined, are nonsensical. Dillon's populism is as comically naive as that of Lou Bergson, another follower of William Jennings Bryan, who argued that populist responsibilities included blowing up Wall Street.[12]

When Dillon became a man obsessed with ideas Trueman held in contempt, their friendship was doomed. Trueman withdrew his money from Dillon's bank, and the rupture was complete. Without the other, each man lost the balance that had made him seem larger than the ordinary: Dillon's talk became shrilly sarcastic; Trueman's silence, heavily grim. Each seemed to become smaller; then each disappeared; Dillon unexpectedly died; Trueman silently left town. From San Francisco came another picture of Mr. Trueman, a sad parody of the largeness and harmony of his former friendship with Dillon. Trueman had taken "an office in a high building at the top of what is now Powell Street," and there he "used to sit tilted back in his desk chair, a half-consumed cigar in his mouth, morning after morning, apparently doing nothing, watching the Bay and the ferry-boats, across a line of wind-racked, eucalyptus trees."

What was lost for the narrator was a picture of equilibrium, a memory of harmony. She is left with the uneasiness of seeking a retreat that no longer exists:

> The breaking-up of that friendship between two men who scarcely noticed my existence was a real loss to me, and has ever since been a regret. More than once, in Southern countries where there is a smell of dust and dryness in the air and the nights are intense, I have come upon a stretch of dusty white road drinking up the moonlight beside a blind wall, and have felt a sudden sadness. Perhaps it was not until the next morning that I knew why,—and then only because I had dreamed of Mr. Dillon or Mr. Trueman in my sleep. When that old scar is occasionally touched by chance, it rouses the old uneasiness; the feeling of something broken that could so easily have been mended; of something delightful that was senselessly wasted, of a truth that was accidentally distorted—one of the truths we want to keep.

The breaking of that friendship "has ever since been a regret," Cather wrote, using again a word that in *Obscure Destinies* expresses the deepest losses: Mrs. Harris regrets her home in Tennessee, Victoria Templeton regrets her youth, and Vickie will regret that she heeded Mrs. Harris so little. In "Two Friends" the narrator too regrets a loss, made more painful when unexpectedly she comes upon "a dusty white road drinking up the moonlight." The description of the earth and the moon pouring their energies into each other is as passionate as any Cather wrote, yet here the experience is of beauty without truth, balance without harmony, sound without meaning.

When I began writing about *Obscure Destinies* I responded most intensely to "Neighbour Rosicky" and "Old Mrs. Harris," tacitly agreeing with critics who regard "Two Friends" as a lesser story. I now believe "Two Friends" belongs in the volume, is one of Cather's strongest stories, and is among the most disturbing of her writing. In this, apparently the most impersonal story in the volume, Cather wrote her most personal account of loss. By recalling a vivid memory that she once thought an unalterable reality "somewhere at the bottom of things," then telling how it was "accidentally distorted," Cather questioned the foundations of the romantic's faith. Truth in the sense Cather meant lies beyond accident (the transcendental romanticism of her early writing) or beneath accident (the archetypal symbolism of her later writing); because it is unalterable, it provides an anchor, a retreat, a breeding ground, "a soft bottom resting place." By considering in "Two Friends" the possibility that this truth can be distorted and lost, Cather anticipated the dark romanticism of her final novels.

Notes

1. *OD.*
2. For identification of models Cather used for characters in *OD*, see Bennett.
3. In this letter Cather was writing specifically about "Two Friends," but her point is a general one. Willa Cather to Carrie Miner Sherwood, 27 January 1934, Willa Cather Historical Center, Red Cloud, Nebraska.
4. *My Ántonia* (1918; Boston: Houghton Mifflin, Sentry Edition, 1961), 18.
5. Walt Whitman, "Song of Myself," stanza 50, 9th ed. (1891–92) of *Leaves of Grass*, in *Complete Poetry and Selected Prose*, ed. James E. Miller, Jr. (Boston: Houghton Mifflin, Riverside Editions, 1959), 67.
6. *O Pioneers!* (1913; Boston: Houghton Mifflin, Sentry Edition, 1962), 309.
7. Whitman, stanza 52.
8. "Katherine Mansfield," in *OW*, 108.
9. For a fuller discussion of the sequence of female narrators in this story, see Susan J. Rosowski, "Willa Cather's Women," *Studies in American Fiction* 9 (Autumn 1981): 261–75.

10. "Katherine Mansfield," in *OW*, 108–10. Again, Cather's comments on Mansfield's stories seem a gloss to "Old Mrs. Harris":

> One realizes that even in harmonious families there is this double life: the group life, which is the one we can observe in our neighbour's household, and, underneath, another—secret and passionate and intense—which is the real life that stamps the faces and gives character to the voices of our friends. Always in his mind each member of these social units is escaping, running away, trying to break the net which circumstances and his own affections have woven about him. One realizes that human relationships are the tragic necessity of human life; that they can never be wholly satisfactory, that every ego is half the time greedily seeking them, and half the time pulling away from them. In those simple relationships of loving husband and wife, affectionate sisters, children and grandmother, there are innumerable shades of sweetness and anguish which make up the pattern of our lives day by day, though they are not down in the list of subjects from which the conventional novelist works.

11. Willa Cather to Carrie Miner Sherwood, 27 January 1934.

12. For a discussion of the relationships between Cather's writing and the Populist movement of the early 1890s, see Robert W. Cherny, "Willa Cather and the Populists," *Great Plains Quarterly* 3 (Fall 1983): 206–18.

Chronology

1873   Willa Cather born 7 December to Mary Virginia (Boak) and Charles Cather, at Back Creek, near Winchester, Virginia, the first of seven children. Later moves to Willow Shade, a large house in mountain countryside that informs her earliest memories.

1883   Moves to Webster County, Nebraska, where paternal grandparents are already settled on a pioneer farm. The following year Charles moves the family to Red Cloud, the town that will figure so prominently in Cather's writing.

1885–90   Attends public schools in Red Cloud, graduating from high school in a class of three in June 1890.

1891   Enrolls at the University of Nebraska, where she spends the first year taking classes to meet the entrance requirements not provided by Red Cloud High School.

1892   Her first published story, "Peter," appears in *The Mahagoney Tree*.

1893   Begins to review plays and books for the *Nebraska State Journal* and remains a regular contributor until graduation. After leaving Lincoln she continues to send pieces to the *Journal*, occasionally also writing for the Lincoln *Courier.*

1895   Graduates from the University of Nebraska.

1896   Moves to Pittsburgh to edit the *Home Monthly.*

1897   Begins regular newspaper work for the Pittsburgh *Daily Leader.*

1898   Meets Ethelbert Nevin, model for the composer in "'A Death in the Desert'" and "Uncle Valentine."

1899   Meets Isabelle McClung, who becomes a lifelong friend. Two years later begins to live at the McClung home, an arrangement that lasts until moving to New York.

1900   "Eric Hermannson's Soul" published in *Cosmopolitan.*

1901 Begins teaching at Allegheny High School. "Jack-a-Boy" published in the *Saturday Evening Post.*

1902 Travels abroad with Isabelle McClung.

1903 *April Twilights*, book of verse, published.

1905 *The Troll Garden*, first book of stories, published.

1906 Moves to New York to work as an editor for *McClure's.* Becomes a trusted colleague and friend of S. S. McClure; eventually writes (pseudonymously) his autobiography (1913).

1907 Spends much of the year in Boston researching the life of Mary Baker Eddy. This work, now recognized as largely written by Cather, was a sensation when serialized in *McClure's.* Meets Sarah Orne Jewett in Boston.

1909 "The Enchanted Bluff" published in *Harper's.*

1910 Meets the writer Elizabeth Shepley Sergeant, who will write a memoir of their friendship.

1911 "The Joy of Nelly Deane" published in *Century.*

1912 "The Bohemian Girl" published in *McClure's.* Leaves *McClure's* to write full-time. *Alexander's Bridge* published. Moves into an apartment with Edith Lewis at 5 Bank Street, her home until 1927.

1913 *O Pioneers!* published. Meets the Wagnerian soprano Olive Fremstad, a friendship important for the stories about opera singers and for *The Song of the Lark.*

1915 *The Song of the Lark* published.

1917 Makes first visit to the Shattuck Inn at Jaffrey, New Hampshire, where she finds congenial working conditions.

1918 *My Ántonia* published.

1920 *Youth and the Bright Medusa*, her second book of stories, brought out by Alfred A. Knopf, thereafter Cather's publisher. Alfred and Blanche Knopf remain trusted friends for the rest of her life. The lead story, "Coming, Aphrodite!," appears in the *Smart Set* under the title "Coming, Eden Bower!" Other new stories also center on opera singers.

1922   *One of Ours* published. Makes first visit to Grand Manan, an island in the Bay of Fundy, where in1927 she will build a summer home.

1923   Receives Pulitzer prize for *One of Ours*. *The Lost Lady* published.

1925   *The Professor's House* published. "Uncle Valentine" published in *Woman's Home Companion*.

1926   *My Mortal Enemy* published.

1927   *Death Comes for the Archbishop* published.

1928   Charles Cather dies. Cather and Edith Lewis forced to leave their Bank Street apartment by area development. They take temporary quarters in the Grosvenor Hotel.

1930   Meets violinist Yehudi Menuhin, then a boy prodigy. Friendship with the gifted Menuhin family will be a source of great pleasure and comfort.

1931   *Shadows on the Rock* published. Virginia Cather dies.

1932   *Obscure Destinies* published. Cather had worked on these three stories in the years since her father's death. Moves to a Park Avenue apartment, her last home.

1935   *Lucy Gayheart* published.

1936   *Not under Forty*, a collection of literary essays, published. Writes "The Old Beauty."

1940   *Sapphira and the Slave Girl* published.

1942   Meets the Norwegian novelist Sigrid Undset.

1944   Awarded the gold medal for fiction by the National Institute of Arts and Letters.

1945–47   Writes "Before Breakfast" and "The Best Years," her last completed stories.

1947   Dies at home on 24 April. Buried in Jaffrey, New Hampshire.

1948   Knopf publishes *The Old Beauty and Others*, Cather's last three stories.

1949   Knopf publishes *Willa Cather on Writing: Critical Studies on Writing as an Art*, a collection of her essays.

1965 University of Nebraska Press publishes *Willa Cather's Collected Short Fiction, 1892–1912.*

1973 University of Nebraska Press publishes *Uncle Valentine and Other Stories: Willa Cather's Uncollected Short Fiction, 1915–1929.*

Selected Bibliography

Primary Works

Short Story Collections

Early Stories of Willa Cather. New York: Dodd, Mead, 1957; Apollo, 1966. "Peter," "Lou, the Prophet," "A Tale of the White Pyramid," "A Son of the Celestial: A Character," "'The Fear That Walks by Noonday,'" "On the Divide," "A Night at Greenway Court," "Nanette: An Aside," "Tommy, the Unsentimental," "The Count of Crow's Nest," "A Resurrection," "The Prodigies," "Eric Hermannson's Soul," "The Dance at Chevalier's," "The Sentimentality of William Tavener," "The Affair at Grover Station," "A Singer's Romance," "The Conversion of Sum Loo."

Five Stories. New York: Vintage, 1956. "The Enchanted Bluff," "Tom Outland's Story," "Neighbour Rosicky," "The Best Years," "Paul's Case," "Willa Cather's Unfinished Avignon Story" (article by George N. Kates).

Great Short Works of Willa Cather. Edited and with an introduction by Robert K. Miller. New York: Harper & Row, Perennial Library, 1989. "Eric Hermannson's Soul," "The Sculptor's Funeral," "A Wagner Matinee," "Paul's Case," "The Enchanted Bluff," "The Bohemian Girl," "Uncle Valentine," "Neighbour Rosicky," "Old Mrs. Harris," "The Novel Démeublé."

Obscure Destinies. New York: Alfred A. Knopf, 1932; Vintage, 1974. "Neighbour Rosicky," "Old Mrs. Harris," "Two Friends."

The Old Beauty and Others. New York: Alfred A. Knopf, 1948; Vintage, 1976. "The Old Beauty," "The Best Years," "Before Breakfast."

The Troll Garden. 1905. Reprinted in *Collected Short Fiction*, 1965. Reprinted and edited with an introduction by James Woodress. Lincoln: University of Nebraska Press, 1983. "Flavia and Her Artists," "The Sculptor's Funeral," "The Garden Lodge," "'A Death in the Desert,'" "The Marriage of Phaedra," "A Wagner Matinee," "Paul's Case."

Uncle Valentine and Other Stories: Willa Cather's Uncollected Short Fiction, 1915–1929. Edited with an introduction by Bernice Slote. Lincoln: University of Nebraska Press, 1973. "Uncle Valentine," "Double Birthday," "Consequences," "The Bookkeeper's Wife," "Ardessa," "Her Boss," "Coming, Eden Bower!"

Willa Cather's Collected Short Fiction, 1892–1912. Edited by Virginia Faulkner with an introduction by Mildred R. Bennett. Lincoln: University of

Nebraska Press, 1965; rev. ed., 1970. Includes stories from *The Troll Garden*. Stories before 1905: "Peter," "Lou, the Prophet," "A Tale of the White Pyramid," "A Son of the Celestial," "The Clemency of the Court," "'The Fear That Walks by Noonday,'" "On the Divide," "A Night at Greenway Court," "Tommy, the Unsentimental," "The Count of Crow's Nest," "The Strategy of the Were-Wolf Dog," "A Resurrection," "The Prodigies," "Nanette: An Aside," "The Way of the World," "The Westbound Train," "Eric Hermannson's Soul," "The Sentimentality of William Tavener," "The Affair at Grover Station," "A Singer's Romance," "The Conversion of Sum Loo," "Jack-a-Boy," "El Dorado: A Kansas Recessional," "The Professor's Commencement," "The Treasure of Far Island." Stories after 1905: "The Namesake," "The Profile," "The Willing Muse," "Eleanor's House," "On the Gulls' Road," "The Enchanted Bluff," "The Joy of Nelly Deane," "Behind the Singer Tower," "The Bohemian Girl." Pseudonymous stories: "The Dance at Chevalier's," "The Burglar's Christmas," "The Princess Baladina—Her Adventure," "The Elopement of Allen Poole."

Willa Cather: 24 Stories. Selected and with an introduction by Sharon O'Brien. New York: New American Library, 1987. "Peter," "Lou, the Prophet," "A Tale of the White Pyramid," "The Elopement of Adam Poole," "The Clemency of the Court," "On the Divide," "A Night at Greenway Court," "Tommy the Unsentimental," "The Burglar's Christmas," "Nanette: An Aside," "Eric Hermannson's Soul," "The Sentimentality of William Tavener," "A Singer's Romance," "The Professor's Commencement," "The Treasure of Far Island," "The Namesake," "The Profile" "The Willing Muse," "Eleanor's House," "On the Gulls' Road," "The Enchanted Bluff," "The Joy of Nelly Deane," "Behind the Singer Tower," "The Bohemian Girl."

Youth and the Bright Medusa. 1920. New York: Vintage, 1975. "Coming, Aphrodite!" "The Diamond Mine," "A Gold Slipper," "Scandal," "Paul's Case," "A Wagner Matinee," "The Sculptor's Funeral," "'A Death in the Desert.'"

Works in Other Genres

Alexander's Bridge. 1912. Lincoln: University of Nebraska Press Bison Book, 1962.

A Lost Lady. 1923. New York: Vintage, 1972.

April Twilights. Poems. 1903. Edited and with an introduction by Bernice Slote. Lincoln: University of Nebraska Press, 1962; rev. ed., 1968; Bison Book ed., 1976.

Death Comes for the Archbishop. 1927. New York: Vintage, 1971.

Lucy Gayheart. 1935. New York: Vintage, 1971.

My Ántonia. 1918. Boston: Sentry, 1954.
My Mortal Enemy. 1926. New York: Vintage, 1961.
O Pioneers! 1913. Boston: Sentry, 1962.
One of Ours. New York: Alfred A. Knopf, 1922.
The Professor's House. 1925. New York: Vintage, 1973.
Sapphira and the Slave Girl. 1940. New York: Vintage, 1975.
Shadows on the Rock. 1931. New York: Vintage, 1971.
The Song of the Lark. 1915. Boston: Houghton Mifflin, 1983.

Nonfiction

The Kingdom of Art: Willa Cather's First Principles and Critical Statements, 1893–1896. Edited by Bernice Slote. Lincoln: University of Nebraska Press, 1966.
Not under Forty. New York: Alfred A. Knopf, 1936.
Willa Cather on Writing: Critical Studies on Writing as an Art. New York: Alfred A. Knopf, 1949; Lincoln: University of Nebraska Press Bison Book, 1988.
The World and the Parish: Willa Cather's Articles and Reviews, 1893–1902. 2 vols. Edited by William M. Curtin. Lincoln: University of Nebraska Press, 1970.

Secondary Works

Biographies, Memoirs, and Other Views of Cather

Ambrose, Jamie. *Willa Cather: Writing at the Frontier.* Oxford and Hamburg: Berg Publishers, 1988.
Arnold, Marilyn. "The Other Side of Willa Cather." *Nebraska History* 68 (Summer 1987): 74–82.
Bennett, Mildred R. *The World of Willa Cather.* 1951; Lincoln: University of Nebraska Press Bison Book, 1961.
Bohlke, L. Brent, ed. *Willa Cather in Person: Interviews, Speeches, and Letters.* Lincoln: University of Nebraska Press, 1986.
Brown, E. K. *Willa Cather: A Critical Biography.* Completed by Leon Edel. New York: Alfred A. Knopf, 1953.
Gerber, Philip L. *Willa Cather.* Boston: Twayne, 1975.
Lee, Hermione. *Willa Cather: Double Lives.* New York: Pantheon Books, 1990.
Lewis, Edith. *Willa Cather Living: A Personal Record.* 1953; rpt. with a foreword by Marilyn Arnold. Athens: Ohio University Press, 1989.

Nelson, Robert J. *Willa Cather in France: In Search of the Lost Language*. Urbana: University of Illinois Press, 1988.

O'Brien, Sharon. *Willa Cather: The Emerging Voice*. New York: Oxford University Press, 1987.

Quirk, Tom. *Bergson and American Culture: Willa Cather and Wallace Stevens*. Chapel Hill: University of North Carolina Press, 1990.

Robinson, Phyllis C. *Willa: The Life of Willa Cather*. New York: Doubleday, 1983.

Rosowski, Susan J. *The Voyage Perilous: Willa Cather's Romanticism*. Lincoln: University of Nebraska Press, 1986.

Sergeant, Elizabeth Shepley. *Willa Cather: A Memoir*. 1953; rpt. Lincoln: University of Nebraska Press Bison Book, 1963.

Thomas, Susie. *Willa Cather*. Savage, Md.: Barnes & Noble, 1990.

Woodress, James C. *Willa Cather: Her Life and Art*. 1970; rpt. Lincoln: University of Nebraska Press Bison Book, 1975.

————. *Willa Cather: A Literary Life*. Lincoln: University of Nebraska Press, 1987.

Critical Studies: Books on the Short Stories

Arnold, Marilyn. *Willa Cather's Short Fiction*. Athens: Ohio University Press, 1984.

Critical Studies: Articles and Essays on the Short Stories

Albertini, Virgil. "Willa Cather's Early Short Stories: A Link to the Agrarian Realists." *Markham Review* 8 (Summer 1979): 69–72.

————. "Willa Cather and Football: A Strange Duality." *Platte Valley Review* 14 (1986):7–18.

————. "Willa Cather and the Bicycle." *Platte Valley Review* 15 (1987): 12-22.

Arnold, Marilyn. "Cather's Last Three Stories: A Testament of Life and Endurance." *Great Plains Quarterly* 4 (Fall 1984): 238–44.

Baker, Bruce. "Nebraska's Cultural Desert: Willa Cather's Early Short Stories." *Midamerica: The Yearbook of the Society for the Study of Midwestern Literature* 14 (1987): 12–17.

————. "'Old Mrs. Harris' and the Intergenerational Family," in *Willa Cather and the Family, Community and History: The BYU Symposium*, edited by John J. Murphy. Provo, Utah: Brigham Young University, 1990.

Bass, Eben. "The Sculptor of the Beautiful." *Colby Library Quarterly* 14 (1978): 28–35.

Bennett, Mildred R. "A Note on . . . The White Bear Stories." *Willa Cather Pioneer Memorial Newsletter* 17 (Summer 1973): 4.

————. "Willa Cather's Bodies for Ghosts." *Western American Literature* 17 (Spring 1972): 39–52.

Blanch, Mae. "Joy and Terror: Figures of Grace in Cather and O'Connor Stories." *Literature and Belief* 8 (1988): 101–15.

Bohlke, L. Brent. "Beginnings: Willa Cather and 'The Clemency of the Court.'" *Prairie Schooner* 48 (Summer 1974): 134–44.

Burgess, Cheryll. "Willa Cather's Homecomings: A Meeting of Selves," in *Willa Cather and the Family, Community, and History.*

Bush, Sargent, Jr. "'The Best Years': Willa Cather's Last Story and Its Relation to Her Canon." *Studies in Short Fiction* 5 (Spring 1968): 269–74.

Carpenter, David A. "Why Willa Cather Revised 'Paul's Case': The Work in Art and Those Sunday Afternoons." *American Literature* 59 (Dec. 1987): 590–608.

Cary, Richard. "The Sculptor and the Spinster: Jewett's 'Influence' on Cather." *Colby Literary Quarterly* 10 (Sept. 1973): 168–78.

Ferguson, J. M., Jr. "'Vague Outlines': Willa Cather's Enchanted Bluffs." *Western Review: A Journal of the Humanities* 7 (Spring 1970): 61–64.

Hall, Joan Wylie.. "Cather's 'Deep Foundation Work': Reconstructing 'Behind the Singer Tower.'" *Studies in Short Fiction* 26 (Winter 1989): 81–86.

———. "Treacherous Texts: The Perils of Allusion in Cather's Early Stories." *Colby Library Quarterly* 24 (Sept. 1988): 142–50.

Kimbel, Ellen. "The American Short Story, 1900–1920," in *The American Short Story: 1900–1945*, edited by Philip Stevick, 51–59, Boston: Twayne, 1984.

Kvasnicka, Mellanee. "'Paul's Case' in the High School Classroom." *Willa Cather Pioneer Memorial Newsletter* 31, No. 3 (Summer 1987): 37–39.

Leddy, Michael. "Observation and Narration in Willa Cather's *Obscure Destinies.*" *Studies in American Fiction* 16, no. 2 (Autumn 1988): 141–54.

Levy, Helen Fiddyment. "Mothers and Daughters in 'The Bohemian Girl' and *The Song of the Lark*," in *Willa Cather and the Family, Community and History.*

Miller, Robert K. "What Margie Knew," in *Willa Cather and the Family, Community, and History.*

Murphy, John J. "Cather's 'Two Friends' as a Western 'Out of the Cradle.'" *Willa Cather Pioneer Memorial Newsletter* 31, no. 3 (Summer 1987): 39–41.

Oehlschlaeger, Fritz. "Willa Cather's 'Consequences' and *Alexander's Bridge:* An Approach through R. D. Laing and Ernest Becker." *Modern Fiction Studies* 32 (Summer 1986): 191–202.

Petry, Alice Hall. "Harvey's Case: Notes on Cather's 'The Sculptor's Funeral.'" *South Dakota Review* 24 (Autumn 1986): 108–16.

Piacentino, Edward J. "The Agrarian Mode in Cather's 'Neighbour Rosicky.'" *Markham Review* 8 (Summer 1979): 52–54.

Rubin, Larry. "The Homosexual Motif in Willa Cather's 'Paul's Case.'" *Studies in Short Fiction* 12 (Spring 1975): 127–31.

Schneider, Sister Lucy. "Land Relevance in 'Neighbour Rosicky.'" *Kansas Quarterly* 1 (Winter 1968): 105–10.

————. "Willa Cather's 'The Best Years': The Essence of Her 'Land-Philosophy.'" *Midwest Quarterly* 15 (October 1973): 61–69.

Sheehy, Donald G. "Aphrodite and the Factory: Commercialism and the Artist in Frost and Cather." *South Atlantic Quarterly* 41 (1986): 49–63.

Skaggs, Merrill M. "Cather's Complex Tale of a Simple Man, 'Neighbour Rosicky,'" in *Willa Cather and The Family, Community, and History.*

Slote, Bernice. Introduction to "Wee Winkie's Wanderings" and an untitled sketch. *Willa Cather Pioneer Memorial Newsletter* 17 (Summer 1973): 2–3.

Stouck, David. "Willa Cather's Last Four Books," in *Critical Essays on Willa Cather,* edited by John J. Murphy, 290–99. Boston: G. K. Hall, 1984.

Summers, Claude J. "'A Losing Game in the End': Aestheticism and Homosexuality in Cather's 'Paul's Case.'" *Modern Fiction Studies* 36, no. 1 (Spring 1990): 103–19.

Wasserman, Loretta. "Willa Cather's 'The Old Beauty' Reconsidered." *Studies in American Fiction* 16, no. 2 (Autumn 1988): 217–27.

————. "Is Cather's Paul a Case?" *Modern Fiction Studies* 36, no. 1 (Spring 1990): 121–29.

————. "Going Home: 'The Sculptor's Funeral,' 'The Namesake,' and 'Two Friends,'" in *Willa Cather and the Family, Community, and History.*

Bibliographies

Arnold, Marilyn. *Willa Cather: A Reference Guide.* Boston: G. K. Hall, 1986.

Crane, Joan. *Willa Cather: A Bibliography.* Lincoln: University of Nebraska Press, 1982.

Index

The Author

Loretta Wasserman is a professor in the Department of English, Grand Valley State University, Allendale, Michigan. She has published on "Sir Gawain and the Green Knight" and on Willa Cather in *Studies in the Novel, American Literature, Modern Fiction Studies,* and *Studies in American Fiction.* Her essay "William James, Henri Bergson, and Remembered Time in *My Ántonia*" appears in *Approaches to Teaching "My Ántonia,"* published by the Modern Language Association. Her degrees are from the University of Minnesota.

The Editor

Gordon Weaver earned his Ph.D. in English and creative writing at the University of Denver, and is currently professor of English at Oklahoma State University. He is the author of several novels, including *Count a Lonely Cadence, Give Him a Stone, Circling Byzantium,* and most recently *The Eight Corners of the World.* His short stories are collected in *The Entombed Man of Thule, Such Waltzing Was Not Easy, Getting Serious, Morality Play,* and *A World Quite Round.* Recognition of his fiction includes the St. Lawrence Award for Fiction (1973), two National Endowment for the Arts fellowships (1974 and 1989), and the O. Henry First Prize (1979). He edited *The American Short Story, 1945–1980: A Critical History* and is currently editor of the *Cimarron Review.* Married and the father of three daughters, he lives in Stillwater, Oklahoma.

WITHDRAWN

DATE DUE